REFUGE RECOVERY

Also by Noah Levine

Dharma Punx

Against the Stream:
A Buddhist Manual for Spiritual Revolutionaries

The Heart of the Revolution:
The Buddha's Radical Teachings on
Forgiveness, Compassion, and Kindness

REFUGE RECOVERY

A Buddhist Path to Recovering from Addiction

Noah Levine

HarperOne
An Imprint of HarperCollins*Publishers*

HarperOne

HarperCollins books may be purchased for educational, business, or sales promotional use. For information please e-mail the Special Markets Department at SPsales @harpercollins.com.

HarperCollins website: http://www.harpercollins.com

HarperCollins®, ♨®, and HarperOne™ are trademarks of HarperCollins Publishers.

FIRST EDITION

Designed by Level C

Library of Congress Cataloging-in-Publication Data
Levine, Noah.
Refuge recovery : a buddhist path to recovering from addiction / Noah Levine.
pages   cm
ISBN 978–0–06–212284–1
1. Recovering addicts—Life skills guides. 2. Religious life—Buddhism. I. Title.
HV4998.L48   2014
294.3'4442—dc23   2013040251

19 20 21   LSC(C)   20

CONTENTS

PART TWO
REFLECTIONS ON RECOVERY

APPENDIXES

PREFACE

Addiction is the repetitive process of habitually satisfying cravings to avoid, change, or control the seemingly unbearable conditions of the present moment. This process of craving and indulgence provides short-term relief but causes long-term harm. It is almost always a source of suffering for both the addict and those who care about the addict.

Recovery is a process of healing the underlying conditions that lead to addiction. It is establishing and maintaining the practice of abstaining from satisfying the cravings for the substances and behaviors that we have become addicted to. Recovery is also the ability to inhabit the conditions of the present reality, whether pleasant or unpleasant.

Renunciation is the practice of abstaining from harmful behaviors.

A **refuge** is a safe place, a place of protection—a place that we go to in times of need, a shelter. We are always taking refuge in something. Drugs, alcohol, food, sex, money, or relationships with people have been a refuge for many of us. Before addiction, such refuges provide temporary feelings of comfort and safety. But at some point we crossed the line into addiction. And the substances or behaviors that were once a refuge inevitably became a dark and lonely repetitive cycle of searching for comfort as we wandered through an empty life.

Active addiction is a kind of hell. It is like being a hungry ghost, wandering through life in constant craving and suffering. Refuge Recovery, the Buddhist-inspired approach to treating addiction, offers a plan to end the suffering of addiction.

Traditionally, Buddhists commit to the path of awakening by taking refuge in three things: awakening (Buddha), truth (Dharma), and community (Sangha). If the teachings and practices offered here resonate with you as true and useful, we invite you to take refuge in this process of awakening, truth, and community. Practicing these principles and developing these skills will lead to a safe place, a true and reliable refuge, a place that is free from addiction, to a full recovery.

Introduction

Refuge Recovery is a practice, a process, a set of tools, a treatment, and a path to healing addiction and the suffering caused by addiction. The main inspiration and guiding philosophy for the Refuge Recovery program are the teachings of Siddhartha (Sid) Gautama, a man who lived in India twenty-five hundred years ago. Sid was a radical psychologist and a spiritual revolutionary. Through his own efforts and practices he came to understand why human beings experience and cause so much suffering. He referred to the root cause of suffering as "uncontrollable thirst or repetitive craving." This "thirst" tends to arise in relation to pleasure, but it may also arise as a craving for unpleasant experiences to go away, or as an addiction to people, places, things, or experiences. This is the same thirst of the alcoholic, the same craving as the addict, and the same attachment as the codependent.

Eventually, Sid came to understand and experience a way of living that ended all forms of suffering. He did this through a practice and process that includes meditation, wise actions, and compassion. After freeing himself from the suffering caused by craving, he spent the rest of his life teaching others how to live a life of well-being and freedom, a life free from suffering.

Sid became known as the Buddha, and his teachings became known as Buddhism. The Refuge Recovery program has adapted the core teachings of the Buddha as a treatment of addiction.

Buddhism recognizes a nontheistic approach to spiritual practice. The Refuge Recovery program of recovery does not ask anyone to believe anything, only to trust the process and do the hard work of recovery.

This book contains a systematic approach to treating and recovering from all forms of addictions. Using the traditional formulation, the program of recovery consists of the Four Noble Truths and the Eightfold Path. When sincerely practiced, the program will ensure a full recovery from addiction and a lifelong sense of well-being and happiness.

Of course, like every path, you can only get to your destination by moving forward, one foot in front of the other. The path is gradual and comprehensive, a map of the inner terrain that must be traversed in the process of recovery. The path includes daily meditation practices, written investigations of the causes and conditions of your addictions, and how to find or create the community you will need in order to heal and awaken. We have also included stories of people who have successfully recovered with the help of Buddhist practices.

Although I am credited with writing the book, the large community at Refuge Recovery is the inspirational and creative force behind it. This community has helped shape, inform, and enhance the program with their direct experience of practicing these principles. This book, then, should be viewed as a collaborative effort, a book written for the plural rather than the singular—the "we" instead of the "I," since it speaks for Buddhists and addicts everywhere.

Lastly, we are aware that more will be revealed. It is our hope that we have offered here a substantial and useful foundation to the Buddhist recovery movement. We have every intention to learn and grow and revise as we go. This is just the first edition. Enjoy!

The Process

Refuge Recovery follows the traditional Buddhist system of the Four Noble Truths, which begin with four actions.

1. We take stock of all the suffering we have experienced and caused as addicts.

2. We investigate the causes and conditions that lead to addiction and begin the process of letting go.

3. We come to understand that recovery is possible and take refuge in the path that leads to the end of addiction.

4. We engage in the process of the Eightfold Path that leads to recovery.

   1. Understanding

   2. Intention

   3. Communication/community

   4. Action/engagement

   5. Livelihood/service

   6. Effort/energy

7. Mindfulness/meditations

8. Concentration/meditations

The core philosophy of Refuge Recovery is based on renunciation and abstinence. We believe that the recovery process truly begins when renunciation is established and maintained. We also understand that imperfection and humility are part of the process. Even when we refrain from the primary drug or behavior, addiction at times manifests in other behaviors. We are not holding perfection as the standard, but as the goal. We believe in the human ability and potential for complete renunciation of behaviors that cause harm. We understand that for many this is an ongoing process of establishing and/or reestablishing renunciation.

Renunciation alone is not recovery, however. It is only the beginning. Those who maintain abstinence but fail to examine the underlying causes and conditions are not on the path to recovery. They are simply stopping the surface manifestations of addiction, which will inevitably resurface in other ways.

The eight factors, or folds, of the path are to be developed, experienced, and penetrated. This is not a linear path. It does not have to be taken in order. In fact, all the factors need to be developed and applied simultaneously. And to truly break free from addiction, the eight folds of recovery must be constantly maintained.

Although the process and sequence of recovery will vary from person to person, the following is an overview of how the Refuge Recovery approach may be applied.

We begin by accepting all the ways that addiction has caused suffering in our lives and the lives of others. Turning inward and acknowledging our suffering is the beginning of the process, but it is also an ongoing practice. On a daily basis, we practice mindfulness of suffering, its causes and its cessation.

Next we investigate the underlying conditions that have influenced, exacerbated, and perpetuated our addictions.

Through reading, listening, studying, and practicing the principles of the Four Truths (which includes the Eightfold Path) we come to understand the possibility and potential of our own recovery. Having some inkling of hope and willingness, we take refuge in the potential of our own recovery (Buddha), the Four Truths and Eightfold Path of recovery (Dharma), and in the community of fellow recovering addicts (Sangha).

We embark on the practice of the Eightfold Path. We encourage you to begin with the practice of meditation right away. Meditation is going to be the most important tool in supporting our renunciation. Begin with the practice of focusing on your breath. After a week, you will alternate forgiveness practice (explained in Chapter 5) with breath practice every other day. Eventually we will want you to learn and practice all the meditations offered, but we encourage you to first develop the meditations that increase concentration.

As your skill in concentration increases, we begin practicing the four foundations of mindfulness and the heart practices of loving-kindness, compassion, appreciation, and equanimity.

Next we refine understanding, intentions, and livelihood. This is a gradual path. No one changes overnight, but we all must continue to practice, study, and act wisely to find the freedom from addiction we seek.

We engage in the relational aspect of forgiveness, making amends to all people we have hurt through our addictions, words, and actions.

Compassionate action is an integral aspect of the path. We encourage you to find ways to be of service, to be generous, and to be kind. Once you maintain renunciation for over a year, establish a regular meditation practice, and complete the inventories, you are ready to become a mentor for newer members.

We will maintain daily meditation practices and relationships with the community of recovering people.

PART ONE

The Four Truths of Recovery

1

Addiction Creates Suffering

The path of Refuge Recovery begins with the First Truth: addiction creates suffering. This is not a philosophy. It is a practice; it demands action. We must understand, acknowledge, admit, and accept all the ways addiction has caused suffering in our lives. We take this action by writing and sharing an in-depth and detailed inventory of the suffering we have experienced in association with our addictions.

You are probably already painfully aware of how addiction leads to suffering. Addiction to drugs, alcohol, sex, people, gambling, money, food, or whatever the addiction creates an almost unbearable amount of suffering, confusion, and harm in the life of the addict and the lives of the people who love the addict.

What usually starts as a search for happiness and pleasure almost always ends in tremendous sorrow, loss, confusion, and suffering. Very often it leads us to suicidal thoughts, despondency, and shame. For the addict in the midst of addiction, life is often a downward spiral that ends in incarceration, institutionalization, violence, loss, and death. Some may continue to function in seemingly normal ways—working, parenting, and participating in society—but an internal death occurs, a numbness arises, and they start to disconnect from themselves and from others. A wall of denial and suppression, too high and too thick to scale or break through, keeps others out and keeps the addict in, trapped by his or her own defenses, prisoner to his or her addictions.

To start the process of healing and recovery from addiction, the first thing we must do is accept how our addictions cause suffering in us and in the ones we love. We begin by understanding that addiction always creates suffering. Suffering is greed, hatred, and delusion. For the addict it may manifest as: Suffering is the stress created by craving for more. Suffering is never having enough to feel satisfied. Suffering is stealing to support your addiction. Suffering is lying to hide your addiction. Suffering is feeling ashamed of one's actions. Suffering is feeling unworthy. Suffering is living in fear of the consequences of one's actions. Suffering is the feelings of anger and resentment. Suffering is hurting other people. Suffering is hurting yourself. Suffering is the feeling of being isolated and alone. Suffering is the feeling of hatred toward oneself or others. Suffering is jealousy and envy. Suffering is feeling less than, inferior, or beneath others. Suffering is feeling superior, better than, or above others. Suffering is greedy, needy, and selfish. Suffering is the thought that *I cannot be happy until I get. . . .* Suffering is the anguish and misery of being addicted.

All these feelings are unnecessary suffering caused by an imbalance between our instinctual drive for happiness and our instinctual need for survival. It is also very important to remember that the end of suffering does not mean the end of pain or difficulties, just the end of creating unnecessary suffering in our lives.

Once we understand this, we can begin to determine whether or not we have crossed the line into addiction, by looking at all the ways that our drug use, drinking, eating, gambling, sex, or relationships have become a source of suffering. This is a process that cannot be skipped or half-assed. The foundation of our recovery is a complete admission and acceptance of the suffering that we caused and experienced due to addiction.

We must do away with any shred of denial, minimization, justification, or rationalization. To recover, we must completely and totally understand and accept the truth that addiction creates suffering. As addicts we have crossed a line we can rarely cross back over: drug addicts and alcoholics almost never regain the ability to drink or use drugs in a nonaddictive way. We have to accept that abstinence is our only hope. (For those who have become addicted to food or certain unhealthy behaviors related to food, however, total abstinence is not an option. Recovery entails abstaining from the addictive behaviors associated with eating to find a balanced relationship to food.)

There is a small percentage of former addicts who, after a period of abstinence and recovery, seem to be able to return to drinking or drugs without losing control, but this is a rare exception. The vast majority of addicts will return to active addiction if they participate in the behaviors or substances that they became addicted to in the past.

Accepting that we are addicts is also accepting that we can no longer drink, or use drugs. When we bring awareness to the addiction and all the suffering it has caused, we begin a process of recovery that will always include abstinence. In the beginning it can be hard to imagine our lives without the drugs or behaviors that bring us temporarily relief from the difficulties in our lives.

But later, after we have firmly established the recovery practices, it will be hard to imagine a life that included addiction. The meditation, ethical behavior, and community involvement that accompany the Buddhist path to recovery will lead to an experience of such contentment and well-being that there will no longer even be an attraction to escaping or creating a false temporary intoxication.

The practice of these principles, which begins with accepting the reality of our addiction, will bring us to an enlightened state, an experience of wisdom and compassion and forgiveness and love for ourselves and everyone else. When we experience this healing, the drive to escape and/or control our experience will be replaced by a deep appreciation of life as it is. As compassion grows in our hearts, pain will no longer be so scary or something to escape from; instead, it will turn into just another sensation or emotion to feel and to meet with kindness. We will once again be able to enjoy the life that we live, with the normal joys and sorrows that come with birth and death.

FIRST TRUTH INVENTORY

Write an in-depth and detailed inventory of the suffering you have experienced in association with your addictions. Share the inventory with a trusted friend, a mentor, or your Buddhist teacher to understand the nature of your addiction/suffering.

On the path of recovery, we must understand that addiction is suffering, and accept all the ways that it has caused suffering in our lives. Only then can we begin to find freedom from addiction. Without full acceptance and disclosure, recovery is not possible. We cannot skip this step; we must be thorough in our inventory process.

This inventory is designed to help the addict acknowledge and accept all the ways that he or she has caused and experienced suffering. It is through the process of understanding, acknowledging, and admitting suffering that we can begin to transform our relationship with suffering and begin to find liberation from it.

Answer each question in depth and detail. It is best to use a notebook dedicated solely for this process. This inventory is also available in worksheet format at www.refugerecovery.org.

Suffering is the stress created by craving for more. List the stress your addiction has created. How did it manifest day to day? Moment to moment?

Suffering is never having enough to feel satisfied. How did you suffer from dissatisfaction?

Suffering is stealing to support your addiction. Did you steal? From whom? Make a thorough inventory of your theft.

Suffering is lying to hide your addiction. When did you start lying about your addiction? Was it blatant? Did you minimize your addiction or omit any details. Whom have you lied to? And what is the extent of your dishonesty?

Suffering is feeling ashamed of one's actions. List all the ways you have felt ashamed or guilty about your actions.

Suffering is feeling unworthy. Has unworthiness affected you? In what ways?

Suffering is living in fear of the consequences of one's actions. Did fear of getting caught affect your life? How?

Suffering is the feelings of anger and resentment. Make a detailed list of everyone whom you have ever been angry or resentful toward and why.

Suffering is hurting other people. Make a list of all the people you have hurt and how you hurt them.

Suffering is hurting yourself. List all the ways you hurt yourself.

Suffering is the feeling of being isolated and alone. Did your addiction lead to a feeling of isolation? At the end, were you all alone in your self-created disconnection? Write about how that felt.

Suffering is the feeling of hatred toward oneself. List all the things about yourself you have ever judged or hated.

Suffering is jealousy and envy. Make a list of everyone and everything you have ever envied.

Suffering is feeling less than, inferior to, or beneath others. List the ways you have felt less than.

Suffering is feeling superior, better than, or above others. List the ways you have felt superior.

Suffering is greedy, needy, and selfish. List how being greedy, needy, and selfish has affected your life and relationships.

Suffering is the thought that *I cannot be happy until I get* . . . What are some of the things you think you need to be happy?

Suffering is the anguish and misery of being addicted. What other forms of misery did your addiction create? How did it affect your sexuality? Your finances? Your looks?

Suffering is greed, hatred, and delusion in all its many manifestations. How else have you suffered?

List the ways you put yourself or someone else in physical danger because of your addiction.

List any grief or trauma in your life that has fueled your addiction.

How have you suffered physically?

List any other emotional suffering you have experienced as a result of addiction.

List the things that have disappeared from your life due to your addiction.

List any misfortunes you have experienced because of your addiction.

List any missed opportunities or failures in your life that were due to your addiction.

List the ways in which your addiction has made your life different from the way you want it or intended it to be.

Look at your relationship history and consider how your addiction may have caused harm in your relationships. Name some of the people and ways that you hurt them.

How has your addiction affected your sex life?

Has your sexual conduct hurt others? Name the people and be specific about how you caused harm.

Are there any other ways that you have experienced or caused suffering in relation to your addiction? List them here. Don't leave anything out.

What would your life look like if you were free from the suffering that addiction has caused? Be specific. Allow yourself to be generous and hopeful.

Where do you see yourself in five years? Ten years? Twenty years?

2

The Cause of Addiction Is Repetitive Craving

We have come to understand that all forms of addiction have their roots in the natural human tendency to crave for life to be more pleasurable and less painful than it actually is. The addict is not at fault for the root causes and conditions that lead to addiction, only for the habitual reactive patterns that perpetuate it.

We are all born into bodies that are ruled by a survival instinct that is out of harmony with reality. The normal state of human beings is a sleeplike state of nonwisdom. The evolutionary process of human beings is dictated by a natural desire to live and to pursue happiness. But our survival instinct, which influences the body and mind, is really just the unrealistic expectation that life is always pleasurable and never painful. Our bodies naturally crave pleasure, which we think equals happiness, safety, and survival. We hate pain, which we think equals unhappiness and death.

The addict is an extreme manifestation of the normal human condition. It is not a lack of morality or any deep character flaw that creates addiction; it is almost always just a lot of pain and a lack of tolerance or compassion for this pain that get us stuck in the repetitive and habitual patterns of drinking, drugging, over-eating, or whatever actions our addictions take. In some cases the underlying causes are not as clear, but the suffering that addiction creates is always obvious and undeniable.

Craving a pleasurable existence is normal. Through our natural lust for pleasure and hatred of pain we will survive for as long as the circumstances and the body's impermanence allow. We need these base cravings to survive. They are not the enemy; they are a necessary function of life. But as we know all too well, a life lived chasing pleasure and running from pain leads only to more and more suffering and, in our case, addiction to the substances or be-haviors that have given us temporary relief.

Our survival instinct does not grant us happiness, only tempo-rary survival. A life based on craving and aversion is a miserable existence, even for nonaddicts, but for the addict it means a life that eventually becomes unbearable.

One of the other very important factors here is the truth of impermanence. We are born into a mind/body process that is constantly changing in a constantly changing world. Everything is impermanent—every pleasure, every pain, every body. But the survival instincts crave permanence and control. The body wants pleasure to stay forever and pain to go away forever. This is the very cause of attachment and aversion. The fact of impermanence leads to a generalized unsatisfactoriness. Many times we are drink-ing, using, or acting out in direct response to the unsatisfactoriness of life. We are trying to escape from it or to create a new temporary reality to replace it.

But the truth is we are all constantly struggling with loss; we are constantly grieving the loss of each experience and trying in vain to create stability out of transience. Addictions are almost always created out of the vain hope to control the amount of plea-sure and pain we experience. We become addicted to pleasant feelings that drugs, alcohol, sex, food, and money temporarily create in us.

The main problem here is that we are addicted to impermanent phenomena.

When we get strung out on impermanent experiences, such as drugs, sex, food, people, places, or things, we are always left with the stress and grief of loss since our intoxication can never last.

When we spend our lives avoiding unpleasant experiences by taking another drink, devouring another chocolate cake, or masturbating for the seventh time today, we are actually causing the unpleasant experiences to last longer than they need to. The unpleasant thoughts, feelings, and sensations are impermanent but also persistent; trying to push them away is futile and always results in stress, anger, and suffering. It is like we create a dam in the flow of experience.

Rather than letting impermanence do its job, we block the passing of the pain. We often do this through suppression, avoidance, ignoring, and self-medicating, or by hardening the heart and shutting out life. But when we sober up, the pain is still there waiting to be felt. Some have been successful in suppressing and denying the pain in their lives for long periods of time, but the dam will always burst eventually. And there is nothing more painful than a lifetime of suppressed pain flooding through all at once.

Aversion is the survival instinct. To survive, we have to hate pain. But aversion doesn't leave us with much freedom or happiness. In our case, aversion leads to addiction. Our instincts tell us to hate pain and to get rid of it as quickly as possible, but our recovery depends on a radical shift in how we respond to those cravings and aversions.

Now, we are not suggesting that you just accept every painful experience that life presents you or that you should never try to avoid pain or seek pleasure. Not at all. What we are saying is that there is lot of unpleasantness about life that is unavoidable. While our instinct is to avoid it all—especially as people addicted to avoidance-producing substances or behaviors—it is impossible to get rid of or avoid all the pain in life. The trick is to avoid what you can. Meditation is one of the tools that will lead to discernment about what pains to avoid and what pains are unavoidable and need to be accepted.

As recovering addicts it is important to enjoy pleasure—as long as it is balanced and appropriate. We will need to find healthy ways to enjoy life. In the beginning of recovery, this can often prove challenging. After the intense sensations of drugs, alcohol, and gambling, the subtle pleasures of a healthy meal or good workout often pale in comparison. Even great sex can seem lacking when compared to a crack binge or heroin run. It may take a while to learn to appreciate and enjoy the simple joys of sobriety and recovery.

As we practice meditation and start to live an ethical life, it will become more and more clear when it is time to accept the pains or enjoy the pleasures and when it is wise to refrain or avoid them. It is possible to live a balanced life, a life that enjoys pleasure without clinging to it, and it's possible to meet the unavoidable pains with tenderness and care. We call this "nonattached appreciation" and "compassionate response ability" and will go into more detail about how to develop these skills in the Eightfold Path. We are not trying to escape the human condition or the pleasures and pains of the human mind/body. Our job is to recover from the self-destructive tendencies of addiction and to live an embodied and fully human life.

THE SECOND TRUTH INVENTORY

Write an in-depth and detailed inventory about the difficulties that you have been trying to avoid. Investigate how craving for more pleasure and less pain led you into addiction. Share the inventory with a trusted friend, a mentor, or a teacher and come to understand the cause of your addiction/ suffering.

Let's look at the source of our sufferings and addictions. Remember that there is a difference between craving and desire. Craving is the thought and feeling that says "I have to have it, I cannot be happy without it." Desire says, "I want it but will be fine with or without it."

Craving for sense pleasures seems to be the most prevalent cause of addiction. Most addicts have deep wells of pain in their past. Their addictions are manifested as ways to avoid or replace the suffering they have been through. Let's look deeply and careful at our lives, to see what may have led to our addiction.

Answer each question in depth and detail. It is best to use a notebook that is dedicated solely for this process. This inventory is also available as a worksheet at www.refugerecovery.org.

What are your most painful memories? Write about what happened and how you have been carrying those memories with you. How did your addictions affect those memories, or how did those experiences affect your addiction?

Are there things that you have been keeping in, secrets or experiences that you swore you would never talk about? Now is the time to let them out; your recovery depends on it.

Was there violence or abuse in your home? What did it feel like to be there?

Were you neglected in any way? What do you remember about that?

Were there any inappropriate sexual experiences in your life? Abuse? Coercion? Rape? Molestation? Objectification? Exposure? What happened?

Is there a family history of addictions/alcoholism? What was is like growing up with that legacy? How did it affect you?

When did you first feel like escaping your reality?

When did you start drinking/using/acting upon what would become your addictions?

When did it become a problem?

What's the thing that you are most afraid of? How did your addiction affect that fear?

Have you contemplated or tried to take your own life in an attempt to be rid of pain? When? What happened? How do you feel about being alive now?

How have addictive behaviors or substances been an escape from the realities of your life?

Are there difficulties in your life you wish to avoid facing? What are they? Is that connected with addictive craving?

What are you attached to? Make a list.

Name some of specific sensory pleasure(s) you crave?

Do you use physical pleasure to avoid pain? How?

Do you intentionally create physical pain to control or avoid emotional pain? How? Cutting? Fighting? Extreme exercise?

How has pleasure seeking caused you suffering? Give some examples.

What could you have done differently when craving, rather than attempting to satisfy it?

What do you think you need to be happy?

What material things do you think would complete you?

How is your happiness tied to your expectations? Do you indulge your addictions when you do get what you want?

How has the craving for success caused you suffering?

Has failure led to relapse?

What would your life look like if you were free from all forms of craving? Take some time to reflect about what freedom would feel like. Remember the end of craving does not mean the end of healthy passions and desires.

3

Recovery Is Possible

Freedom from the suffering caused by addiction is attainable, if we are ready and willing to take responsibility for our actions and to follow the Eightfold Path. As you enter this process and attend group meetings, you will connect with many others who have also suffered the consequences of addiction and are now recovering. Allow the group to inspire you and to show the possibilities of recovery, while also making room for the imperfections of some of the individuals within the group.

The good news is that we can fully recover from addictions. We can end all the unnecessary suffering that our addictive behaviors have created. We can heal and forgive. We will learn to love ourselves and others through the power and practice of Refuge Recovery (Dharma). What we are recovering is not the ability to drink or use drugs or engage in the other behaviors. We are recovering a lost or forgotten part of ourselves. Some call this our true nature or our original goodness. Within each one of us is the potential for wisdom and compassion that has been obscured and buried by our cravings and addictions.

The path of recovery, as outlined here, allows us to slowly, but surely, begin to uncover and directly experience liberating insights and transformative wisdom. When we come to recovery, our minds and hearts are polluted with resentment, anger, fear, judgment, demands, lusts, and ignorance. The process of recovery will slowly transform us, stirring up all our impurities, bringing all the muck to the surface, where it can finally be healed. This is a path that heals the heart and transforms the mind, leaving us with an "awakened heart and mind." We have always had good hearts. They were just so badly covered and obscured they were lost to us. By returning to this lost aspect of ourselves, we recover.

Many would call this a spiritual awakening, enlightenment, or liberation. Although it may be all these things, it is also just a simple psychologically based process of seeing clearly what is true and, then, learning how to respond appropriately. The appropriate response ends suffering. The appropriate response allows us to recover our freedom.

All living beings have the ability to live life along these lines. No one lacks the ability, only the willingness, to take on such a radical task of transformation. Addicts who do not recover are not broken or lost; they just have not yet found the willingness to take this path of wisdom and compassion. We believe in the human capacity for change.

We understand it from direct experience.

If we can, you can.

And we have, so you shall too.

We know that this may be hard to accept at first. Eventually you will know the truth of recovery directly, and you will develop verified faith in the process, based on your own direct experience. Until that time, we encourage you to trust the process, practices, principles, and community.

Just after the Buddha's final awakening, he reflected on what had led to his recovery of wisdom and compassion. He listed five qualities that he had developed. The first thing that he listed was faith or confidence. He said that although he had no guide, no proof, no certainty, what he did have was confidence in his own ability and in the possibility of human liberation. He went on to list effort, mindfulness, concentration, and wisdom as the other factors necessary in the process of recovering our forgotten potential. The path of Refuge Recovery includes all the qualities the Buddha utilized.

We know that this is a difficult thing to ask of addicts who have, very often, been through a long-term demoralizing struggle. We are also sensitive to our core promise that this is not a faith-based process. Refuge Recovery does offer an experiential-based approach, but to get started you have to have at least an inkling of faith, confidence, and hope.

All the proof we can offer you is our own experience. We are a large group of recovering addicts who have successfully used the Buddhist practices to recover.

We invite you to take refuge in the potential of your own recovery/awakening (Buddha), these Four Truths (Dharma), and the group of people who have offered you this book and those whom you will surely meet and connect with as you begin to create and attend Refuge Recovery meetings (Sangha).

Taking refuge is a simple practice that you can begin as soon as you have read through all of the material and have a good understanding of what is being offered and asked for.

When you are ready, after reflecting for a few moments on your own sincere and wise desire to recover, repeat the following phrases:

"I take refuge in the potential of my own recovery" (Buddha).

"I take refuge in the Four Truths and Eightfold Path of recovery" (Dharma).

"I take refuge in the community of fellow recovering addicts" (Sangha).

4

The Path to Recovery

Welcome to the rest of your life. You are entering a way of life that may be familiar to some and will be foreign to others. The Refuge Recovery program is a systematic approach to training our minds to see clearly and respond wisely to life. This is a path that will need to be walked, one foot in front of the other, one breath at a time. In the beginning, some of it may seem confusing or counterintuitive. And some of it is. But you will find that with time, familiarity and experience, it will all make perfect sense and will gradually become a more and more natural way of being.

The Fourth Noble Truth sets out the way, the Eightfold Path, that leads to the end of suffering and is composed of eight factors. The Eightfold Path can be further simplified into three sections:

The first section is Wisdom, which means a wise understanding (1) of reality and wise intentions (2) with our life's energy.

The second section is Ethics, which includes communication/ community (3) actions/renunciation (4) and livelihood/ service (5).

The third section is Meditation. This consists of effort (6), mindfulness (7), and concentration (8).

Each factor of this path is a practice. You will be taking on these eight areas of practice. This is often taught with the analogy of an eight-spoke wheel. You could think of these eight areas of practice as the spokes on your wheel of recovery. Addiction causes a deep imbalance in the wheel of life. The suffering we experience could be seen as the wobbles and thuds of a wheel with missing spokes or at least those not properly connected or out of balance.

A full recovery will take place when all eight spokes are strong and balanced or "true." This will take some time, but it begins as we commit to renunciation, take refuge, and begin the practice of meditation.

Again, it is important to understand that these factors are not a linear progression of one through eight. For most it will actually be the sixth, seventh, and eighth factors of effort, mindfulness, and concentration that will be the key to coming into an authentic wisdom and integration of the other factors.

As we apply our energy and effort (6) to concentrating (8), the mind, and being mindful (7), we begin to see more and more clearly. Mindfulness (7) will lead us to direct understanding. Understanding (1) will lead to wise intentions (2) and actions (4). Mindfulness will also help lead us to appropriate communication (3) and livelihood (5). Eventually, through wise actions and meditations of mindfulness, kindness, compassion, concentration (8), and forgiveness, we will come to directly know that our wheel of life is coming into more balance. With balance will come freedom from craving the substances or behaviors of our addiction.

This Eightfold Path leads to safety, to a refuge from addiction.

1. **Understanding.** We come to know that everything is ruled by cause and effect. The Four Truths are an ongoing practice.

In this step, we gain insight into the impermanent, unsatis-factory, and impersonal nature of life. Forgiveness is possible and necessary.

2. **Intention.** We renounce greed, hatred, and delusion. We train our minds to meet all pain with compassion and all pleasure with nonattached appreciation. We cultivate gener-ous, kind, and compassionate wishes for all living beings. We practice honesty and humility and live with integrity.

3. **Communication/Community.** We take refuge in the com-munity as a place to practice wise communication and to support others on their paths. We practice being honest, wise, and careful with our communications, asking for help from the community, allowing others to guide us through the pro-cess. We practice openness, honesty, and humility about the difficulties and successes we experience.

4. **Action/Engagement.** We purify our actions, letting go of the behaviors that cause harm. The minimum commitment necessary for the path toward recovery and freedom is renun-ciation of violence, of dishonesty, of sexual misconduct, and of intoxication. Compassion, nonattached appreciation, generos-ity, kindness, honesty, integrity, and service become our guid-ing principles.

5. **Livelihood/Service.** We try to be of service to others when-ever possible, using our time, energy, and resources to help create positive change. We work toward securing a source of income/livelihood that causes no harm.

6. **Effort/Energy.** We commit to the daily disciplined practices of meditation, yoga, exercise, wise actions, kindness, forgive-ness, generosity, compassion, appreciation, and the moment-

to-moment mindfulness of feelings, emotions, thoughts, and sensations. Through effort and energy we develop the skillful means of knowing how to apply the appropriate meditation or action to the given circumstance.

7. **Mindfulness/Meditations.** We develop wisdom through practicing formal mindfulness meditation. This leads to seeing clearly and healing the root causes and conditions that lead to the suffering of addiction. We practice present-time awareness in all aspects of our life. We take refuge in the present.

8. **Concentration/Meditations.** We develop the capacity to focus the mind on a single object, such as the breath or a phrase, training the mind through the practices of loving-kindness, compassion, and forgiveness to focus on the positive qualities we seek to uncover. We utilize concentration at times of temptation or craving in order to abstain from acting unwisely.

5

Understanding

We come to know that everything is ruled by cause and effect. The Four Truths are an ongoing practice. In this step, we gain insight into the impermanent, unsatisfactory, and impersonal nature of life. Forgiveness is possible and necessary.

We understand that recovery begins when we renounce and abstain from all substances or addictive behaviors regardless of the specific substances we have become addicted to. Forgiveness, nonharming actions, service, and generosity are a necessary part of the recovery process. We can't do it alone; community support and wise guidance are an integral part of the path to recovery.

First things first. STOP. Abstain, Renounce, Refrain, Quit, Let Go. If you can do it on your own, good. If you need to go to a detox or treatment center, do that. But if you haven't already, it is time to stop. Everything. In some ways, this is the hardest part. In other ways, it's the easiest. Either way, it is the beginning of the path to recovery. We must understand this first.

The Eightfold Path provides the tools to succeed in this process of recovery. There is hope. All we need to do is take the appropriate actions.

CAUSE AND EFFECT

The core of what we need to understand is the importance of cause and effect, and how changing our actions will lead to a change in the outcomes of our lives. This is especially pertinent for the addict, who has been stuck in a habitual, reactive pattern of actions that only result in suffering. The cause of our suffering has always been our reaction to the thoughts, feelings, cravings, and circumstances of our lives. The cause of our addictions has always been the indulgence in the behaviors or substances.

The cause of our recovery will always be our abstinence from those behaviors or substances. Of course this should be clear and obvious. To create health and balance we first have to abstain from the behaviors and substances that have created such a deep imbalance and so much suffering in our lives.

Some may argue against renunciation and abstinence from all intoxicants, saying that the alcoholic should only have to abstain from alcohol and the drug addict from drugs. There are several reasons why we ask for complete abstinence, renunciation, and sobriety.

Most addicts find that their addictive behaviors continue on with the new substances without a full renunciation of all recreational mood and mind-altering substances. It's the phenomenon of switching addictions. It is more common than not. The alcoholic will often end up smoking marijuana addictively; the marijuana addict will often become an alcoholic.

What seems to be true about addicts is that it's not the substances that are the issue. The real problem is the addict's underlying imbalance, which is most likely expressed in compulsive and addictive behaviors with other substances and at times manifests in relationship to work, exercise, food, or sex.

Of course for food, sex, and other behavior-based addictions, abstinence is not always possible. We understand that setting one's own bottom-line behavior will have to suffice, but we still encourage behavior-based addicts to abstain from drugs and alcohol. For this form of treatment to work, mindfulness has to be firmly established. And it is not possible to be fully mindful while intoxicated. As we will discuss in more detail later, mindfulness demands sobriety and a clear mind. This is the other reason why we encourage complete abstinence. To fully benefit from the Eightfold Path, mindfulness is a necessity.

In the long run, all who follow this path diligently will directly experience the satisfaction and joy of a life based on wisdom and compassion. Drugs, alcohol, and compulsive behaviors have no place in the life of a sincere spiritual aspirant.

Eventually, we will look back on our previous life of indulgence as adults look back on the ignorance of their youth, without judgment or condemnation but with a healthy sense of regret and compassion for the previous delusions.

Understanding cause and effect, or what is more familiarly known as karma, goes beyond just abstaining from intoxicants and compulsive behaviors; it applies to all our intentional actions. It is as simple as this: all positive intentional actions have a positive effect on us. All negative intentional actions have a negative effect on us. Recovery comes from positive actions alone.

When we act negatively, we seek refuge in our addiction to avoid the consequences of those negative actions. When we act in positive ways, however, we create positive feelings of well-being and balance within us, which allows us to cut through our addictive habits.

Here is a simple way to look at it.

Positive actions that have positive results:

Honesty

Generosity

Kindness

Humility

Compassion

Forgiveness

Patience

Nonviolence

Renunciation

Nonattachment

Mindfulness

Appreciation/Gratitude

Negative actions that have negative results:

Dishonesty/Stealing

Selfishness/Greed

Unkindness/Ill Will

Conceit/Self-Esteem

Hatred/Resentment

Impatience/Demanding

Violence/Harmful Speech

Gluttony/Indulgence

Intoxication

Sexual Misconduct

Jealousy

Clinging/Attachment/Controlling

Delusion/Confusion/Unawareness

To recover, we have to create the causes for recovery, to begin living more and more in the positive and less and less in the negative. We don't have to become perfect over night, but we do have to strive for progress and balance on a daily basis.

Understanding the Four Truths is at the heart of this aspect of the path.

1. We suffer due to our addictions and the general difficulties of being human in this world of constant change and loss.

2. Craving is a natural phenomenon; it is not all our fault, but we are fully responsible for our healing and recovery.

3. We can fully recover and enjoy a life of sanity and well-being.

4. This is the path.

IMPERMANENCE

One of the key things to understand is that everything is constantly changing, both inside and outside of us. Our very bodies are in a constant state of change. First we grow up, then we grow old, then we die and our bodies continue to change and decay. On the physical level this is obvious to most. But mentally it can come as breaking news.

All sensations, emotions, sounds, smells, tastes, sights, thoughts, feelings, moods, experiences, and relationships are impermanent. They all have a beginning, a middle, and an end. Nothing lasts, nothing is constant, nothing is permanent—just the rising and passing of phenomena in the body. As we all found out as addicts, it is impossible to maintain a permanent state of intoxication. That was not our failure as addicts. It wasn't because we weren't smart or rich enough. It was because it is impossible to win the battle against impermanence.

Of course, the fact that life is impermanent can also be good news. It can work to our advantage. "This shit won't last forever," for instance. Impermanence is primarily problematic when life is pleasurable. Even when we are enjoying ourselves, we still have to understand "this shit won't last forever." If we live long enough, we will watch all our friends and family go through losses, illnesses, and difficulties and eventually die. Many of us have already experienced tremendous amounts of loss at young ages. We live in a world of loss, of change, of constant instability.

To recover we must understand and accept impermanence. We must replace the reactive survival instinct of clinging, grasping, and attachment with the wise response of nonclinging, nonattachment, and compassion. In a world where everything is constantly being pulled beyond our grasp, clinging and grasping always result in the rope burns and unnecessary suffering that accompanies it.

UNSATISFACTORY

At the first glimpse of insight into impermanence, people usually wonder, "If everything's always changing, where can we find lasting happiness?" The answer is simple. Once we stop looking for happiness in impermanent things, we begin to find an internal source of happiness that is not dependent on or addicted to circumstances. As we accept the unsatisfactory nature of all conditioned phenomena, we begin to seek the unconditioned source of all happiness. This is what the Third Truth points to; what we uncover or recover is the liberated heart of unconditional freedom.

IMPERSONAL

Another aspect of the human condition that we will come to understand directly, through the practice of mindfulness, is that a lot of what's happening is not so personal. This will be revealed on several levels. First, that we have probably been self-absorbed for most of our lives: thinking about ourselves, obsessing about our place in the family, the community, the world; letting our pleasure or pain rule our lives. Even the codependent who may say, "I haven't been self-centered, I've been centered on others," will, upon closer examination, have to admit that his or her caretaking and enabling arose from a deep place of craving a pleasant outcome. The codependent too is being driven by self-centered craving. To not let others suffer or struggle, when suffering or struggling is appropriate or necessary, is selfish of the enabler. Because enablers can't tolerate someone else's pain, they create situations and relationships that prolong and, at times, increase the suffering.

Almost every addict has been living a self-focused, self-centered, self-indulgent, and selfish life. Of course there may be an exception here and there. Maybe you were the only altruistic junkie on the planet.

What we must recognize is that the self-centeredness of the addict is just an extreme example of a universal human condition. Everyone is self-centered; we are born that way. Our minds and bodies have evolved over thousands of years with a built-in survival instinct that is both inwardly and outwardly focused.

Humanity's self-centered craving and fear-based mentality is not the fault of the individual. It's not personal; it's just part of being human. Being self-centered is not our fault, but it is our responsibility to find a balanced and informed relationship with our self-centered tendencies.

As we have already proven with our experiences, a life lived with unchecked and untreated selfishness is doomed to result in a downward spiral of more and more suffering and alienation. We are all born into a dysfunctional system. We are wired with an ancient survival instinct that was created to keep us safe from predators on the savanna. We needed to fight for our lives for the survival of our species. We needed to be on constant alert for the next danger, the next attack. Although most of us are no longer in danger of being eaten, or attacked, we still live with the evolutionary biology of a scared animal.

FORGIVENESS

Underlying most addictions is a deep well of pain. The pain of our lives has been caused by people and circumstances that have hurt us. We have usually responded with resentment, anger, and hatred toward the cause of our pain. The more we hate, the more we create layers of suffering and confusion on top of our pain. All this pain and suffering gives addicts more and more reasons to crave the substances or behaviors that temporarily distract them from or alleviate this pain. As we have already learned, pain is unavoidable, but suffering can be eased by meeting our pain with compassion rather than hatred.

This brings us to the necessity of forgiveness. We can learn to meet the pain of our lives with care and compassion, but we first have to embark on the process of forgiving ourselves and others for all the harms we have experienced and caused.

Forgiveness is a process that continues throughout our lives. It begins when we begin to understand how to forgive. The practice of forgiveness has three aspects or categories.

1. Asking for forgiveness from those whom we have harmed (through both meditation and amends)

2. Offering forgiveness to those who have harmed us (meditation)

3. Forgiving ourselves for all the ways we have harmed ourselves and others (meditation and living amends)

The practice of forgiveness is done in meditation through the repetition of phrases of forgiveness. When we ask for forgiveness, we say one of the following:

"I ask for your forgiveness."

"Please forgive me for having caused you harm."

"I now understand that I was unskillful and that my actions hurt you, and I ask for your forgiveness."

When we offer forgiveness, we can say:

"I forgive you."

"I forgive you for all the ways that you have caused me harm."

"I now offer you forgiveness, whether the hurt came through your actions, thoughts, or words."

"I know you are responsible for your actions, and I offer you forgiveness."

And when we offer ourselves forgiveness, we say:

"I forgive you."

"I forgive you for all of the ways that you have caused me harm."

"I now offer you forgiveness, whether the hurt came through my actions, thoughts, or words."

"I know I am responsible for my actions, and I offer myself forgiveness."

Of course we can't just say the phrases or do the meditation a couple of times and be done with it. We can't just decide to forgive and magically let go of all the past pains and resentments. But it has to begin somewhere, and it begins with the *understanding that all harm caused comes out of suffering and ignorance.*

There is no such thing as wise abuse or enlightened harm. This is the core truth of harm: it always comes from confusion. Anger, violence, and all forms of abuse and betrayal are always motivated by ignorance or confusion. When the mind is clear, however, it is incapable of intentionally causing harm. The awakened mind acts with only wisdom and compassion.

That understanding of harm has crucial implications for us as we practice forgiveness. It forces us to distinguish between the confused, suffering actors and the actions themselves. This is perhaps the most essential understanding in forgiveness: the separation of actor from action. Whether the harm that requires forgiveness was an unskillful act that we carried out, hurting someone else, or an unskillful act on the part of another that we felt victimized by, we must see that the act and the actor are not the same thing. Most of the time the anger and resentment we hold is directed against the actor; in our minds, we don't separate the abuser from the abuse. But this is exactly what we must do. We must come to the understanding that confusion comes and goes. An action from a confused and suffering being in the past doesn't represent who that being is forever; it is only an expression of that being's suffering. And if we cling to resentment over past hurts, we simply increase our own suffering. By holding on to our anger and resentments, we make our own lives more difficult than they need to be.

At the same time we also understand cause and effect, and we know that everyone is fully responsible for their actions. We don't have to punish; everyone is already fully accountable for what they have done.

Some actions may not be forgivable, but all actors are. There is always the possibility of compassion for the actor, the person whose own suffering has spilled onto other people. There is always potential for mercy toward the suffering and confused person who hurts another.

To recover, we must clearly see that we have been in a lot of pain for a long time and that our pain has affected others. Then we can begin to see that the people toward whom we have been holding resentment had also been in pain and that they had spilled their pain onto us. This allows us to separate the person from the action and finally see the confused human being behind his or her hurtful act. This may be the hardest part: not associating the people with their actions, but seeing them as confused human beings trying their best and failing miserably, just as we may have at times.

Most of us have found that having a compassionate attitude toward everyone in our life is incredibly challenging. It may take years of trying and failing to come to a real sense of this understanding.

That's a common experience, because forgiveness can't be forced. Having held on to anger and resentment for so long, we have allowed that reaction to become our habit. And habits take time and intentional action to break.

Through forgiveness, we retrain our mind and heart to respond in a new and more useful way. By separating the actor from the action, we get to the root of the suffering, both caused and experienced. This is a counterintuitive process. Our biological instinct is to respond to all forms of pain with aversion, anger, hatred, and resentment, the basic survival instinct of the human animal. It works quite well to protect us from external harm, yet it seems to create an even more harmful inner experience. The process of forgiveness is the process of freeing oneself from internal suffering.

But forgiveness is not just a selfish pursuit of personal happiness. For addicts, it is a necessity for our recovery. If we don't forgive, we will never maintain abstinence. Resentment will lead to relapse, over and over, again and again.

The great thing is that this not only leads to healing in ourselves, it alleviates suffering in the world. As each one of us frees ourselves from resentments that cause suffering, we simultaneously relieve our friends, family, and community of the burden of our unhappiness and the wreckage of our addictions. This is not a philosophical proposal; it is a verified and practical truth. Through our suffering and lack of forgiveness, we tend to do all kinds of harmful, hurtful things. We close ourselves off from love out of fear of further pains or betrayals. To forgive may leave us feeling vulnerable, but you will come to see that it is perfectly safe, even liberating, to be vulnerable.

A common feeling among many of us who have felt injured by others is that forgiveness is a gift that the offender has not earned. Yet does our lack of forgiveness really punish them, or does it just make our hearts hard and our lives unpleasant? Is forgiveness a gift to others or to oneself?

When it comes to forgiving ourselves, we are both the giver and the recipient of the gift. We are stuck with ourselves for a lifetime, so we might as well find the best way of understanding and accepting the pains of the past. It is in our best interest—and the most beneficial thing we can do for others too—to meet ourselves with compassion rather than resentment. Though this sounds simple and straightforward, forgiving oneself is often the most difficult and most important work of one's lifetime.

It helps if we investigate our mind's tendency to judge and criticize ourselves, paying special attention to any feelings of unworthiness or self-hatred. If we can bring a friendly awareness to our mind's fears and resentments, we may discover that our minds are actually just trying to protect us from further harm. The barrage of fears and insecurities may be a psychological defense system, an attempt to avoid future harm—a confused attempt, of course, because resentment and anger toward oneself never lead to happiness.

But if we can understand and accept that we have been confused, we may find it easier to begin to meet ourselves with mercy and forgiveness, responding to the judging mind with the kind of gentle patience and understanding that we would show a sick and confused friend.

While some resentments seem to vanish forever, others certainly come and go. The most important thing to remember is that we must live in the present, and if in the present moment we are still holding on to old wounds and betrayals, it is in this moment that forgiveness is called for. The experience of forgiveness may be temporary; more may be revealed. If and when that happens, we have the tools to forgive again and again.

The truth is, the experience of forgiveness is a momentary release. We don't and can't forgive forever. Instead, we forgive only for the present moment. This is both good news and bad. The good part is that you can stop judging yourself for your inability to completely and absolutely let go of resentments once and for all. We forgive in one moment and get resentful again in the next. It is not a failure to forgive; it is just a failure to understand impermanence. The bad news is that forgiveness is not something that will ever be done with; it is an ongoing aspect of our lives and it necessitates a vigilant practice of learning to let go and living in the present.

6

Intention

We renounce greed, hatred, and delusion. We train
our minds to meet all pain with compassion and all
pleasure with nonattached appreciation. We cultivate
generous, kind, and compassionate wishes for all living
beings. We practice honesty and humility and live with
integrity.

We intend to meet all pain with compassion and all pleasure with
nonattached appreciation, to be generous and kind to all living
beings, to be honest and humble, to live with integrity, and to
practice nonharming.

Our intentions are always based on our understanding. Therefore, it is important, first and foremost, to understand cause and
effect. Wise intention means that we take full responsibility for all
our actions and the consequences of our actions. In this factor of
the path we are asked to intentionally align our actions with kindness, compassion, generosity, forgiveness, and understanding.

Intentions are the goals or aims of our actions. They are the reasons behind our actions.

Having learned the truths of existence, we must now align our thoughts and intentions toward the goal of recovery and freedom from suffering. This consists of redirecting our thoughts and intentions from the negative karma-producing intentions like greed, hatred, and delusion to the positive intentions of kindness, compassion, generosity, forgiveness, appreciation, and understanding.

In order to recover, we must aim our life's energy and actions toward being free from all forms of hatred, ill will, aversion, and wishing harm on ourselves and others. We must also be free from the greed for pleasure, which is clearly the cause of much of our addictions. Greed is desire out of control. Our intention doesn't need to be free from desire itself, but only free from the extremes of craving, clinging, attachment, and greed. *Wanting* something is not a problem, but *having to have* something is—it's a setup for suffering.

Intention plays a central role in the spiritual life. All our volitional actions come from our intentions—the actions that are at the heart of karma, which literally means *action*. Most of us misunderstand karma: we think that it refers to the result. Something bad happens and we say, "That was my karma" or "That was her karma." Actually, karma is action itself. The result is the karmic fruit. And that karmic fruit—the outcome of an action—comes from our intention, not the act itself. For instance, if we accidentally kill an insect by walking down the street, there is no negative karma created because it was not our intention to kill. But when we volitionally kill insects because we are afraid of them or because we hate them, we commit an intentional act, which bears a negative karmic fruit.

This is an important distinction: karmic results come from our positive or negative intentions, not from the actions themselves. From this perspective, a person can even harm or take human life accidentally—that is, without negative intention—and not have karmic repercussions. There is much confusion about this. In our culture, for instance, there is the saying "The road to hell is paved with good intentions." From a Buddhist perspective, however, this, of course, cannot be true. But the saying comes from the commonly used excuse "That wasn't my intention" or "I had only good intentions, but it was a real mess anyway." This is like the addict who hurts everyone around him or her and then says, "It wasn't my intention." It may be true that the intention was not maliciously hurtful, but if we look at the true motivations and intentions, they were certainly not wise or skillful.

The intention of the addict is usually a selfish craving for pleasure or to escape pain. From the intention of self-serving, often fear-based and dishonest actions comes all the harm that the addict causes. So he or she is fully responsible for all the intentional actions that have resulted in harming others.

Another perhaps more simple example is when we say something, trying to be funny, but it offends someone who is listening. Perhaps we tell a racist joke or say any number of things that some might find funny while others only take offense. We are still fully responsible for our intentions. In humor, our intention may be a selfish motivation to get attention, and some lack of mindfulness that what we are saying may offend someone. But this is not karma-free. We certainly do not intend to be kind, generous, caring, or compassionate when we say mean things just because they might get a laugh. We are often intentionally being mean.

The road to hell and very often relapse, or perhaps relapse and then hell, is not paved with good intentions, quite the opposite. If we bring mindfulness to our motivations and intentions, we will see more and more how we create suffering or end suffering.

This is not to say that actions that come from wise and skillful intentions never cause harm. There are certainly cases where harm will arise from even totally wholesome intentions. For instance, when the enlightened Buddha began to teach that a higher power was not necessary for spiritual practice and awakening, many people were offended and very angry with him—as they may be with us. But the Buddha's intention was one of compassion and care. He only wanted to guide people on a truly transformative path. He saw all the delusions that religious people held and wanted to warn them that they were headed down a dead end. He spoke out of wisdom (truth) and compassion.

There are two levels of intention. The first is simply having the appropriate intention. This means training our mind in thoughts that are free from craving and ill will. It means trying to think about the welfare of all beings. This sort of intention may be as simple as paying attention to our motives and abstaining from actions that are motivated by greed, hatred, or delusion. For example, when we are angry and lashing out at someone, that is obviously an aversive reaction, an intentionally harmful act.

As recovering addicts we must be very careful about our intentions. We have lived lives of intentionally escaping pain and creating pleasure. The habitual pattern that we have set up is to indulge every craving that arises. As we abstain from the behaviors and substances of our addictions, the intention to avoid pain will still be in place until we have trained our minds and bodies in tolerance and understanding. This will come in time through our meditative practice. In the beginning of our recovery, we will have to acknowledge that our intentions are often unwise and based in old patterns of craving pleasure and avoiding pain. We may never get completely free from these instinctual drive-based feelings and intentions. We will, however, become more and more skilled at not taking them personally or acting from the unwise intentions of greed or hatred. Instead, we respond wisely.

The second level of intention goes beyond simply responding wisely to negative thoughts. Here we begin to intentionally cultivate positive thoughts, thoughts of loving-kindness, compassion, appreciation, generosity, patience, tolerance, mercy, and forgiveness. We attempt to use our mental faculties to think about, to consider,

to reason, to reflect, and to apply spiritual principles. We intentionally train our minds to think thoughts that are focused on spiritual
matters rather than material ones.

This second, or higher, level of thought is the proper use of
intentional thinking. Most of the time our minds are preoccupied
with how to get our next fix or, at the least, how to avoid pain or
failure. On this higher level of spiritual thought, we intentionally
think about generosity and compassion. We ask ourselves, *How can
I help?* Or *What is the kind thing to do in this circumstance?* Or *How
can I best express my appreciation and gratitude?* And when someone
offends us, we turn the mind toward compassion, acknowledging
the pain, and then thinking about what it must be like to be in the
mind state of the person who has offended us. We remain mindful
and vigilant about what is going on in our minds. What are we
thinking? What are our intentions?

The first level of intention involves practicing nonharming. It
is simply damage control. But this damage control is key in the
recovery process. For addicts to maintain abstinence and continue
to recover, they will have to align their core conscious motivations
with nonharming. Although this may take some time and constant
vigilance, eventually it will become more and more natural. All
who strive to have more positive intentions and actions report an
increased level of happiness, contentment, and well-being. When
we are happy, we are more likely to maintain recovery.

The second level involves intentionally using our minds to break
free from suffering and dissatisfaction. In this higher aspect of
intention, we use our minds—we in fact *train* our minds—in the
practice of meditation, reflecting on impermanence and on how addiction and grasping create suffering.

So part of our intentional practice is to overcome identification
with negative thoughts through renunciation. When we let go of,
or renounce, ill will and the satisfying of craving, we cut off suf-

fering at its root causes. Renunciation is not about pushing something away; it is about letting go. It's facing the fact that certain things cause us pain, and they cause other people pain. As addicts, we know this better than most. Renunciation is a commitment to let go of the things that create suffering. It is founded on the intention to stop hurting ourselves and others.

For example, when we realize that our craving for pleasure and hatred of pain has become an addiction to drugs and alcohol, we renounce all forms of participation in intoxication. By letting go of drugs and booze, we are left with the raw emotions and fears that had been fueling the addictions. But by facing the aversion to, and fear of, those emotions, and the craving for the insensibility of intoxication, we come to understand that the craving and addiction were mostly in our minds, and that we have the ability to choose, one moment at a time, not to run away from pain by drowning it in false pleasure. Eventually it becomes clear that, as the Buddha taught, pain is not the enemy but just another given aspect of life.

When we accept the inevitability of unpleasant experience, we become willing to tolerate pain and establish a more constructive relationship to pain. In this sense, pain can be seen as being similar to fire. Fire is a natural and useful thing. It heats our homes and cooks our food. But if handled inappropriately, it can also burn the house to the ground. Pain is also useful: it is part of our survival instinct; it tells us when our bodies are in danger or hungry or cold. This works out okay when you can just turn on the AC and cool down. But the survival instinct also knows that too much pain will kill us, so it meets most unpleasant experiences with aversion, fear, and craving for them to go away. And when the pain we experience is emotional or chronic, out of control, the craving for it to go away begins to burn us, consuming us with hatred and resentment.

Aversion to pain is a natural phenomenon, however, and if we have a wise relationship to the mind, it is not a problem at all. Thus it is not about pushing these thoughts and feelings away or pretending we don't experience them. It is about training the mind to not let the fire burn us. That is renunciation. We have the choice to no longer stick our hands in the flames.

Having a positive intention is a protection against relapse and a life of miserable addiction.

We will eventually come to realize that acting out our hatred only causes more hatred. Picking up the burning ember of ill will to throw at our enemy burns us before it burns them. Likewise, when we pick up the substance or behavior that allows us to temporarily avoid the pain, we play with fire. It may feel warm and fuzzy at first, but it will inevitably burn us to the core.

Perhaps most important, we must relax and realize that recovery comes with time. What is true here and now is that we have finally found a secure and reliable refuge. We are now on the path, however gradual it may be, that will lead to a full recovery.

Learning to cultivate the right intentions and thoughts is one of the most important aspects of our recovery. This perspective will unfold with practice. Simply thinking about it isn't enough; we must practice it. The redirection of our intention comes more alive when we develop the moral and ethical practices of nonharming that follow in the next factors of the path.

With the gathering of the attention in the formal practice of mindfulness meditation (7), our mind gets concentrated (8) and our awareness penetrates the truth of what is happening in the here and now. We directly experience and understand (1) the impermanent and dissatisfactory nature of our negative thoughts and we begin to see that they are not as personal as we thought.

You'll remember that wisdom, the first level of the Eightfold Path, is composed of understanding and intention. It is said that trying to comprehend understanding (1) and intention (2) without ethical conduct (3, 4, 5) and the training of meditation (7, 8), the final two levels of the path, is like trying to row a boat across a river without untying it from the dock. It is like trying to row upstream without any oars. Those who try will just get swept away by their addictive tendencies, confusion, ill will, and self-serving tendencies.

7

Communication/Community

We take refuge in the community as a place to practice wise communication and to support others on their path. We practice being honest, wise, and careful with our communications, asking for help from the community, allowing others to guide us through the process. We practice openness, honesty, and humility about the difficulties and successes we experience.

COMMUNITY

A central and integral aspect of the recovery process is being involved in community. It is our hope that Refuge Recovery will provide that community for you. But if it doesn't, perhaps because there is not a program yet in your area, we implore you to find communities that can offer refuge. Many of our members have found great support in 12-step communities and/or Buddhist communities while trying to build the support of a Refuge Recovery group. If a group doesn't exist in your area, we encourage you to start one.

Having a community to practice with is important on several levels: as recovering addicts we need like-minded people to guide us, to inspire us, to support us, and to challenge us when we get stuck. The Buddha felt that community was so important that he included it in the traditional ritual of "taking refuge," or committing to the path of freedom. Committing to that path, dedicating our life to recovering our Buddha nature, consists of committing to *awakening* (Buddha), understanding the *truth about reality* (Dharma), and participating in *community* (Sangha).

From the perspective of recovery, we need communities that include every type of recovering addict. Those with more time and experience become our "mentors" in what the Buddha referred to as "spiritual friendships," guiding us on the path to recovery and inspiring and encouraging us to do the hard work. The more wisdom and compassion those spiritual friends have, the more compassion and kindness they show to us and others. In addition to helping us understand reality and respond with compassion, the wise beings who are our mentors urge us to continue on the path of recovery when it gets difficult and we feel like giving up. This support for abstinence and recovery in a world that conspires to keep us asleep is an invaluable aspect of any sincere desire to recover.

The experienced members of the Refuge Recovery community can serve as mentors, challenging and supporting us in the places we get stuck. They can also act as sounding boards for newly recovering addicts as they work toward new insights and healing. Those members of the community with less experience in recovery can also be of valuable service. Those who are difficult can be our greatest teachers; they help us see clearly where we are on the path. This is made clear to us through our ability to respond with understanding and friendliness to those who need us or who push our buttons. Difficult personalities are a mirror for the places where we get stuck in judgment, fear, and confusion.

Since the freedom we seek is a relational freedom, a state of awareness, skillful actions, and communication that is connected to and in relationship with others, community allows us to put into practice wisdom and compassion toward all beings—even the people we might not necessarily gravitate toward naturally.

COMMUNICATION

Our guiding principle is the nonharmful use of communication. Having firmly established the correct view, understanding (1), thought, and intention (2) about the path to recovery, we must then align our actions (4) with these intentions. This includes realizing the power of communication (3) to cause harm or to bring about positive change and happiness.

When we have wise intentions, we abstain from speaking harmful words. The Buddha classified speech that is harsh, malicious, vain, untrue, or gossipy as being a harmful misuse of communication. Being wise and careful about what we say, write, and otherwise communicate will help us in our process of recovery, and it will build a safe and welcoming community.

A good basic guideline for our communication is to reflect on whether what we are saying is true, useful, kind, and appropriately timed. There may be times when we are honest in what we say, but our words are too brutal or harsh. And there may be other times when we are deliberately being kind with the words we choose, but what we are saying is not totally true. Rigorous honesty is our core intention, but we also must pay attention to the timing of our delivery and whether or not it is even useful to say. Sometimes it is best to wait for a private moment with someone to tell them a difficult truth. If we just blab the truth in front of others, it may be inappropriate or unkind.

We all know the consequence of dishonesty. When we lie, we live in fear of being caught or with the guilt of misleading others. Many of us have spent our lives making up stories about who we are and where we came from. Those lies build on one another until we don't know what we have told to whom. When we come to the path of recovery, it takes some time and much intentional practice to learn to be rigorously honest with ourselves and others.

Harsh speech has been the habit of many of our members for most of their lives. We have always loved the power and shock value of swearing. For some of us even years into recovery, our vocabulary hasn't changed much, but our intentions have changed a lot. Some of us stop swearing altogether and others still swear quite a bit, but now the use of swear words serves more as an exclamation point to illustrate our sentiment than a sword drawn to cause harm. It is our feeling that swearing isn't always harsh or malicious. Like everything else, though, it depends upon our intention—in this case, our intention in using the language.

There is also a difference between talking about someone who isn't present with the intention to cause harm or with the intention to share concern. Most of us have felt the effects of gossip, or the "he said, she said" game. When we look at our intentions behind gossiping, we often realize that we seek power through sharing information. This is not a useful form of communication.

Now, though many of us still get caught up in gossiping, we can bring mindfulness to what it feels like and what our motivations are. This can help us become more aware of the negative consequences it may have.

As far as being on the receiving end of gossip, it can be wise to take on the attitude that anything people say when we are not present is none of our business. That piece of advice can save us from a lot of suffering.

Basing our communication on the principle of kindness is key. What the kind thing to do is will change from situation to situation. And kindness does not always mean it will feel good to say or to hear. Sometimes we have to say things out of kindness even though we know our words will hurt someone's ego or feelings.

The Buddha spoke of the inevitability of praise and blame, fame and disrepute, pleasure and pain, gain and loss. Here it is important to accept that while some will offer praise, others will place blame. Once you begin the recovery process, you will find that some people will be very happy for you and praise you for being in recovery; others will be critical and blame you for selling out, or giving in . . . like when they say, "Recovery is for quitters."

Practicing speech that is true, useful, kind, and appropriately timed is our intention as recovering addicts. In our meetings and meditation groups, we have the opportunity to practice communicating with one another. When we gather, we share our struggles and successes with others, discussing the difficulties we encounter as well as how our recovery is progressing. Humility is very important when we speak about our recovery, to stay open and honest, while also staying right-sized. While we are in recovery we need to be able to strike a balance between not allowing our ego to do all the talking and not letting our low self-esteem to only present what is wrong with us.

Remember that all intentional acts have a karmic consequence (wise understanding, intentions, actions). This includes every form of communication. As we bring mindfulness to our thoughts and feelings, we will begin to see more and more clearly what our true motivations and intentions are. With clarity of intention comes renunciation; with renunciation comes wise communication. This whole process takes applied effort. And will lead to freedom from addiction and all other forms of suffering.

8

Action/Engagement

We abstain from all substances and behaviors that could lead to suffering. We practice forgiveness toward all people we have harmed or been harmed by, including ourselves, through both meditative training and direct amends. Compassion, nonattached appreciation, generosity, kindness, honesty, integrity, and service are our guiding principles.

When we commit to recovery, we must have a personal dedication to purify our actions from the things that cause harm. The minimum commitment necessary for the path toward recovery and freedom is renunciation of violence, dishonesty, sexual misconduct, and intoxication. This is not just for the sake of nobility; it is connected to our understanding of cause and effect (karma).

Mindfulness is a must if we want to be aware of and present with the emotions that provoke harmful actions. First and foremost, an awareness of our inner experience—which includes thoughts, feelings, preferences, emotions, conditioning, and sensations—requires a mind that is free from the obscuring effects of intoxicants. Mind and mood-altering drugs such as alcohol, marijuana, narcotics, barbiturates, and hallucinogens cloud the mind and create an inability to be mindful and fully present for the inner experience. It is clear that the recovery process requires a sober and drug-free mind. (This restriction would not apply to the prescribed psychotropic medications that some people need in order to function skillfully in the world.)

Some addicts may complain that they should be able to continue to indulge if they themselves were not addicted to a particular substance. Take the alcoholic who wishes to smoke marijuana, or the heroin addict who wishes to drink alcohol.

While recovering addicts may find reason to complain about this abstinence-based approach, it is ultimately necessary, because we are taking on a way of life that demands clarity and mindfulness. We follow in the footsteps of the Buddha, and he was clear about the necessity of a fully sober mind in order to awaken and recover our true nature. Yes, this approach asks a lot of us. And it is also promises a lot. Not just a return to the normal suffering of the nonaddict's life, but a spiritual awakening, a life of freedom from suffering altogether.

TOLERANCE AND COMPASSION

From the foundation of a clear, sober mind, we can train ourselves to respond to pain with compassionate investigation and refrain from actions, such as retaliation or self-harm, that will only lead to more suffering. Through our practice of mindfulness, we learn more and more about how to tolerate discomfort, unpleasantness, pain, and sorrow. As we become skilled at tolerating and investigating pain, we will be less likely to act in ways that are harmful. Eventually we will come to understand that compassion is always the appropriate response to all painful experiences, and we will learn to meet all the pain in our lives and in the world with loving-kindness and compassion. This is developed through mindfulness and the heart practices.

NONVIOLENCE

As we commit to nonviolence on every level of existence, we find that the world seems to become a safer place. Many addicts have lived a life of violence and abuse, if not physically at least emotionally. Many of us come from backgrounds of neglect and trauma. For some, violence is all we have ever known, a necessary survival instinct to fight our way out of the hellish situations we were in. We understand this and have lived it too. And we have found that a nonviolent way of life is much more conducive to recovery, perhaps even a necessity. It will take time and probably years of imperfection in this realm, but eventually the recovering addict can and will establish a life of nonviolent actions.

There are many levels to violence and many subtleties to nonviolence. For most, not killing is the most obvious and easiest form of nonviolence. But when asked to include animals, fish, insects, and all other sentient beings in the vow of nonviolence, many resist, sometime violently. We also understand that we live in a world with a food chain and that some level of killing is unavoidable in order to survive. We know that even a vegan lifestyle kills insects and earthworms in the production of vegetables. We do not ask for perfection. It is impossible to go through life without harming anything. But we ask for a sincere attempt to minimize the amount of harm we cause. We try to abstain from intentionally killing.

Then there is fighting, the nonlethal physical violence. Many addicts have found themselves in the occasional street brawl or bar fight, throwing dishes across the dining room, or perhaps slapping their children or spouse. When we have no tolerance for pain and no patience with discomfort, we may strike out at others. When we have little or no control over our emotions, we can be involved in physical violence over and over again. As part of the purification of our actions (karma), we turn toward nonviolence. No more fighting, hitting, or spitting. This does not, however, prohibit us from participating in sports or other physically aggressive activities, such as martial arts, boxing, roller derby, and slam dancing.

Although it takes a more indirect form, the way we communicate with the world can be another form of violence, one that we experience on a daily basis as both spectators and participants. Harsh speech, dirty looks, obscene gestures, and offensive texts and e-mails are also subtle forms of violence. Our communications have power, the ability to cause harm or harmony—it all comes back to our intentions and actions.

We don't have to become perfect to recover, but we must try to abstain from creating more negativity in our lives.

Violent actions have negative karmic consequences, and that karma could manifest as the guilt, shame, or self-hatred that may lead us to relapse, so we abstain from all forms of violence to support our recovery.

HONESTY

As addicts, many of us had to lie and steal to cover up our addictions. Many of us were lying and stealing even before we became addicts. And, for some, lying and stealing was part of what we were addicted to. As we commit to recovery, we commit to honesty. The path of recovery demands honesty. You're unlikely to have much success in recovering if you can't even begin to tell the truth.

Recovery begins when we honestly admit to our addictions and then make the conscious commitment to abstinence. Without honesty the recovery process cannot truly proceed. Some people may be able to maintain periods of abstinence while continuing to lie, cheat, and steal, but most will find that the karma of dishonesty will catch up with them in the forms of guilt, shame, and remorse. And this will often lead to relapse. We are trying to rebuild our lives, the lives torn apart by addiction. To build a solid foundation for our future, for a life of wisdom and compassion, dishonesty must be abandoned.

Stealing has many forms and connotations. There is the obvious "cash register" definition, which means to blatantly steal money or material goods from people. For most of us, this is not a huge problem. For some, however, greed and selfishness are so strong that this form of stealing is a major temptation. Then there are the less obvious forms of stealing, like taking more than your share of something that was freely offered—for example, you pocket a few extra sugars at the coffee shop to bring home with you, or you steal the pen at the bank, or you line your pockets with plastic bags at the buffet and take an extra meal home with you.

Then there are the nonmaterial forms of stealing. For example, some people try to steal all our attention; they are the attention vampires who suck the life out of us, the self-centered people who constantly corner us and try to take us hostage into their personal dramas. We all know people like this, and many of us have probably been guilty of the same thing. How many times have you stolen someone else's time and energy?

Lying can also take different forms. There is the outright lie—intentionally saying something that is false. Then there is embellishment—intentionally exaggerating or overselling something: the big fish stories; the "I-had-a-$2,000-a-day-habit" tall tales.

Then there is the diminishing lie, when we tell only the partial truth or we lessen the severity of it (the "I-only-did-it-a-couple-of-times" line, or the "I-only-lost-a-little-money" partial truth, or the "It-wasn't-that-bad" qualification).

Then there are the lies of omission. These are the true events or thoughts that we simply don't share. Perhaps you fail to tell your spouse about how much money you spent or how much you earn, or you fail to mention you had lunch with an ex. Lies of omission allow us to delude others into believing something that is not true. Or allow them to believe something about us that is not so.

All dishonesty has karmic consequences, and that karma could lead us to relapse, so we abstain from all forms of dishonesty to support our recovery.

REFRAINING FROM SEXUAL MISCONDUCT

Most addicts who come into recovery have some wounds regarding sexuality. Sex is a powerful natural human energy. When we approach sex in a healthy way, it can be a source of great connection and joy. When we approach sex in an unhealthy way, however, it becomes a deep source of suffering. Some of our members have become addicted to sex; others have forsaken it altogether. For the sex addict, creating one's own healthy ideal, bottom-line behaviors and parameters will be necessary. For the rest of us, the simple guidelines of honesty and integrity in our sexual relationships are sufficient. This means refusing to engage in sexual activity with people who are in committed relationships with others, refraining from cheating on our partners, and only engaging in sexual activity with people who are age-appropriate and willing participants. This is all basic, common ethical behavior. But many addicts turn from drugs, alcohol, or other addictions to sex as their next fix. And when sex becomes recreational, people start to lose sight of ethics and responsibility. For many, periods of abstinence or celibacy will be part of the recovery process. Sometimes stepping away from sex altogether is necessary to heal.

But, in general, our attitude toward sex is: go for it as consenting adults—but you also need to accept the consequences. Enjoy all the pleasure and intimacy that sex brings, but be awake. Remember the truth of impermanence: that you are going to change and your partner is going to change and you are probably not going to like it. Be willing to suffer the consequences of impermanence and go into it with your eyes open. All relationships end; even happily-ever-after ends in death and loss.

FORGIVENESS

Forgiveness is an action, the act of letting go of hatred and ill will toward others. We have explored the process and understanding of forgiveness in the first factor of the path. But this is where we put our understanding into action. A regular and consistent practice of the forgiveness meditation will be necessary. Even just ten to fifteen minutes a day of asking for and offering forgiveness in your meditation will train your mind and heart to let go and allow you to be free from the suffering of resentment.

For addicts it is necessary to take forgiveness a step further. While doing the inner work of letting go, we must also take direct relational action. The process of releasing the heart's and mind's grasp on past pains and betrayals almost always includes taking responsibility, by making amends and offering forgiveness when it is appropriate and welcomed. Very often this includes communication with those whom we have harmed, as well as those who have harmed us. This direct communication is the relational aspect of forgiveness. Making amends is a healing and generous act.

This in no way means that we have to reconcile with people who have harmed us. Or that we should subject ourselves or others to further abuse. Part of the forgiveness and healing process is to create healthy boundaries. We may forgive someone but choose never to interact with that person again. We must not confuse letting go of past injuries with feeling an obligation to let the injurers back into our life. The freedom of forgiveness often includes a firm boundary and loving distance from those who have harmed us. We may likewise need to keep a loving distance from those whom we have harmed, to keep them from further harm. To that extent, this practice of letting go of the past and making amends for our behavior is more internal than relational: we can let individuals back into our hearts without ever letting them back into our lives.

You have the list of people you have harmed and been harmed by from the First Truth Inventory. Take another look at it and, with the guidance and support of your mentor, begin making amends for your behavior.

ACTION AND ENGAGEMENT GUIDING PRINCIPLES

As recovering addicts we are embarking on a spiritual path. This path consists of being wise and compassionate in our attitudes and actions. Through meditation, participation in community, and practicing of the principles outlined in the Four Noble Truths, we will come into integrity and become honest and trustworthy again. Kindness will become our guiding principle.

The way that we use the term *kindness* is in the context of what will end suffering and help us to recover in each situation. The next kind action depends on the circumstances. The kind thing to do is the skillful response in each given moment. For instance, when it comes to pleasurable experiences, the kind relationship to pleasure is always nonattached appreciation. If we can enjoy the pleasurable moments without clinging to them or getting caught in the craving for them to last forever, then we can avoid the typical suffering we often create around pleasure. So the kind thing to do is not to get attached. And if we were not able to meet the pleasure with nonattached appreciation, and if we have already become attached, then the kind thing to do is let go, which may mean a practice of renunciation or abstinence.

And the next level of kindness that is often called for is patience with ourselves as we learn to let go. So then patience becomes another act of kindness. And when our minds start judging us for not being very good at letting go, we respond with forgiveness. Forgiveness then is also an act of kindness. Get the picture? The kind thing to do depends on the situation.

When it comes to painful experiences, the kind thing to do is to meet experience with compassion. Compassion ends suffering. It does not end pain, but it does take care of the extra level of suffering we tend to layer on top of our pain. And in that way the kindest thing we can do is to cultivate tolerance and compassion toward pain.

One of the situations where kindness becomes tricky is when we are faced with the possibility that our seemingly kind actions could actually be causing some harm, that we could be enabling someone to suffer more through our intentions to be kind. For instance, in the case of dealing with a friend or family member who is actively engaged in addiction. At some point in the relationship, a strong boundary is going to have to be set. While lending money to a friend in many cases could be seen as a generous and kind act, with the addict it could actually cause more harm than good. Most of us face this dilemma on some level or another on a regular basis, when asked for money on the street by someone who appears to be homeless and intoxicated. Is giving in a way that may very well lead to further addiction and suffering actually an act of kindness at all? In some cases the kindest thing we can do may be to say no. Sometimes kindness means telling individuals the truth that they may not want to hear. At times kindness may even hurt. Kindness doesn't ever have the intention of causing harm, but perhaps in some situations it is just unavoidable. Most of the time our kindness will be felt and appreciated; most of the time people will come to love, appreciate, and feel safe around us due to our commitment to kindness.

All our actions are important and pertinent to our recovery and spiritual awakening. As we become honest with ourselves, others will experience the joy of blamelessness. As we forgive ourselves and others and make amends to those we have caused harm, we will come to know the peace of mind and heart that is the happiness of debtlessness and freedom from ill will. When we are wise and careful with our sexuality, we create both internal and external safety. By not causing harm to ourselves or others, we create a solid foundation for our recovery.

9

Livelihood/Service

We try to be of service to others whenever possible, using our time and energy and resources to help create positive change. We try to secure a source of income/ livelihood that causes no harm.

As addicts, most of us have been selfish and self-centered. When we try to establish this new way of life, we have to go against our selfish tendencies and turn toward a life of compassion and service.

Each new member in a Refuge Recovery group gives us plenty of opportunities to be of service. He or she will need the support of the community. Offering our time and energy to help one another recover is one of the foundations of our program. Mentoring others through the Four Truths will give us the opportunity to be of service, which helps both the mentor and the mentee. Being a mentor helps us break away from our selfish and self-centered tendencies. As we set aside some of our time and energy to show others the path of recovery, we too benefit from that act of generosity.

Being a mentor is a great responsibility. It means not only teaching but also showing through our actions what it means to be in recovery. We mentor each other in the way we speak in meetings and the way we practice meditation on a regular basis.

Through talking with one another and establishing a community, we see that every one of us is experiencing the same things. At heart, everyone has resistance to pain and attachment to pleasure. As we saw observed in the First Truth, suffering is a universal facet of human existence. We all suffer, but suffering takes on a magnified form in the addict. So the pain in life is a given that we all have to deal with, but if we respond in a destructive way, as an addict does, we add extra suffering and dissatisfaction on top of that pain. As we recover we begin to see that it is true for everyone, both addicts and nonaddicts alike.

Once we have acknowledged how much suffering we've experienced in our lives, and once we have clearly seen how much suffering there is in the world, the only rational response is an engaged compassion toward all forms of suffering. As recovering addicts we must commit our life's energy to creating positive change.

The compassionate response is both natural and cultivated. It is a natural outcome of our deliberate internal transformation, an intentional choice to use our life's energy to free ourselves from confusion and to help others get free from confusion as well. We need to learn to respond with friendliness and compassion not only to our own pain but also to that of the world.

For us as addicts, the necessity of transformation is too pressing to wait until a genuine compassionate understanding develops. Perhaps we have already been reacting with anger in an attempt to change the world. Anger is a very understandable and natural reaction to pain. But anger, which is motivated by fear, is also a source of suffering. If we want to eradicate suffering, it makes sense to start with our own. But we don't have to wait until we are free from suffering to take positive action in the world. As our meditation practices develop and our perspective transforms, the anger becomes compassion. Outwardly, the difference may be minimal, but inwardly, the difference between acting out of anger and acting out of compassion is huge.

Helping other recovering people in our community is wise and noble, but let's not stop there. We should also continue to try to be of service outside of our meetings, groups, and communities, getting involved in social, political, and environmental causes close to our hearts. As compassion grows in us, we will want to be more and more engaged in helping to create a positive change in our communities and society and on the planet.

The transformation from a selfish motivation (*I need to do this for myself*) to a more altruistic one (*I dedicate my life's energy to the benefit of all beings*) is a gradual one for most. It will come with time spent helping in the community, as well as through meditative experience.

Knowing that we have the ability to help each other recover and alleviate suffering, we need to bring that intention into the forefront of all our endeavors. This is done by fostering a sincere and altruistic motivation.

To this end, in recovery we may begin to say something like, "May my life's energy be of benefit to all beings. May I be of service to my recovery community. I commit my life's energy to wise and compassionate work."

The Buddha talks about altruistic motivation as a prerequisite to enlightenment in the Eightfold Path when addressing our livelihood. Not only do we have to use our livelihood or life's energy in a way that is nonharming to really be free; we also have to take it that extra step and do something positive, helping one another along the way. This does not mean that we have to stop our chosen career and become a social worker or dedicate ourselves to feeding the starving masses. For many of us, that something extra may be just a shift in attitude and motivation in whatever we are doing, wherever we are in our lives—a shift toward the intention to respond to each person we meet with more caring, more kindness, and more understanding; a shift toward being more compassionate and wise with our life's energy.

Although our motivation to help others may be sincere, it is important to acknowledge that it may not always be 100 percent altruistic. There is often a mixed motivation for serving. Sometimes it feels as if we have to serve in order to forgive ourselves for the harm we have caused and the negativity we have created. Such a response could be motivated by guilt, but it could likewise come from a healthy sense of regret and a commitment to karmic purification. At other times we may be motivated to serve out of a desire to look good—to *appear* altruistic and thereby gain praise.

If we feel a drive to use all our life's energy to serve, it is essential that we be clear about our motivation, even and especially when it is selfish. Serving feels good. We like the experience of getting out of our self-centered thoughts and feelings by focusing our attention on doing good for others. We gain love and respect from those we help. But we must constantly be reminded that, as the Buddha has been rumored to have said, "We could search the whole world and never find another being more worthy of our love than ourselves."

In other words, the truest altruism is to include oneself at all times, making sure that our intention is to serve *all* beings, not just others.

Once we have found some level of ease and well-being in life, due to our spiritual practice and recovery, we don't get to just relax and enjoy it. Knowing that the happiness and freedom we have found in life are very much a part of the fact that we've committed to serve all beings with our life's energy and not expend it in selfish pursuits, we continue on that path as a natural course of action, doing all we can to bring about positive change to this world. The path of the recovery is a path of service. On this path we have many tools: education, resources, protection from harm, and the ability to inspire meditative transformation.

Our mindfulness meditation practice—our formal and informal training—develops insight into all the ways that we create suffering. That wisdom is liberating, but it is only one wing of recovery. The other wing is compassion. For most, some level of wisdom must be developed before true compassion can be uncovered. Then our care, generosity, understanding, and skillful response to suffering are genuine. Without kindness and compassion, wisdom is lacking; it is imbalanced. It takes caring and understanding for a fully recovered heart to soar to freedom.

For many, this will lead to wanting to find a profession that causes no harm and, if possible, one that is of service. Now that we are living with the knowledge of cause and effect (karma), we can't spend our time and energy in a job that causes harm to people, animals, or the planet. This would be counterproductive to our goal of recovery and awakening.

Our livelihood also impacts karma: since all intentional actions have reciprocal outcomes, the time we spend on the job is a major generator of karma. It doesn't work to practice spiritual principles at home while earning a living through something that creates harm in the world. By participating in a harm-causing career, we not only hurt other beings or our world, we create future harm for ourselves. Some of the traditional jobs to avoid are killing living beings, selling living beings, selling weapons, selling intoxicants, and making money in the sex industry. All these jobs create suffering and confusion on some level. So even if the easiest way we find to make money is through selling booze or drugs, we need to choose different work. If we profit from substances that cause confusion and suffering, we are actually committing an act of self-sabotage.

If our job is, say, bartending, close attention to our intention may reveal that our work is motivated by greed. A bartender witnesses the suffering of alcoholism and the confusion of drunkenness, yet profits from that suffering. Because profiting from the suffering and confusion of others has a negative karmic consequence, those who wish to be free from suffering should try to avoid all such jobs.

In recovery, we must be committed to what is most beneficial—not what is easiest. Remember: we have set our intentions to go against the stream. It is not the easiest way, to be sure, but it is perhaps the only way to achieve freedom and bring about positive change.

For those who find themselves stuck, at least for the meantime, in a job that is not in line with our nonharming intentions, it will not help to be judgmental, defensive, or despondent about the situation. Do your best to show up and be mindful of what you are doing. Be as kind as possible to yourself in the process and, when you can, try to find a means of livelihood that is more suitable to your recovery.

Many of our members have had successful recoveries while still engaged in a less-than-optimal livelihood. As a group, we hold no judgment about what one does for a living; our only agenda is recovery. We know from direct experience that being engaged in work that causes harm will often lead to relapse or keep one's recovery stagnant. All our members who have eventually transitioned into more skillful professions have reported an increased level of happiness and greater feelings of contentment. This, in turn, leads to less craving for escape and therefore ensures one's recovery.

Service and wise livelihood are our guiding principles, and they are an integral part of our recovery path. Together we will create a positive change in our lives, society, and the world.

10

Effort/Energy

We commit to the daily disciplined practices of meditation, yoga, exercise, wise actions, kindness, forgiveness,
generosity, compassion, appreciation, and moment-to-
moment mindfulness of feelings, emotions, thoughts,
and sensations. We are developing the skillful means
of knowing how to apply the appropriate meditation or
action to the given circumstance.

Recovery is an act of intentional redirection of our life's energy.
This is where the intentional application of energy comes into play.
Everything we have talked about so far takes effort. None of these
practices or principles are easy to develop. We all have the energy
necessary for this, but only with wise and intentional use of that
energy—that is, with *effort*—can we master these liberating practices and avoid the habitual reactive tendencies that create more
addiction and suffering in our lives.

Some of the ways we must use our energy and effort include
avoiding the things that create suffering, replacing harmful
thoughts and actions with thoughts and actions that create well-
being and peace, developing wisdom and compassion through

meditation and wise actions, and sustaining the wisdom and compassion that arise through careful attention.

When it comes to training our minds and hearts in the path of recovery, each of us must find the balance of applying the right amount of effort: not so much that we get strained, not so little that we get spaced out. Developing a balanced effort and energy in our spiritual life is key to our recovery. We will offer some basic guidelines for how much time and energy to put into meditation, but ultimately everyone will have to find their own balance with these practices. The image of a stream works well for the implied effort that it takes to recover from addictions. In the beginning, we are all floating downstream, following the currents of our cravings and habitual patterns. At some point, we become aware that the currents are dragging us down and that we are no longer free to choose whether we drink, use drugs, gamble, eat, or have sex to excess. We then realize that we have become addicted and that life is passing us by. We can no longer reach the shore, and the undertow grows stronger and stronger.

In the beginning we may have had the illusion of safety. Perhaps we were floating along on a raft or even a yacht. But addiction destroys our craft and leaves us floundering, drowning in the stream of addiction. We eventually wake up and realize that we have to stop; we have to find a way to get back all that we have lost. We want to go back, to return to sanity, to recover.

So we turn to the spiritual practices of Refuge Recovery. The Four Truths give us the tools to start going against the stream. Refuge Recovery is a reliable raft, one filled with people just like you who are also turning around the direction of their lives. In the early days and months of recovery, it can be a struggle simply to stop floating down the stream in the old habitual ways. Relapses may be part of your experience. Just stopping and staying stopped takes a lot of effort. There we are, flailing away in the middle of the stream, and we're doing nothing but trying to stop going downstream with the current. Then, when we renounce and become abstinent, we're stopped, but that's all; we haven't begun to make progress in the other direction yet, because we're in the center of the stream, trying to swim against the current. If we put too much effort into it, we feel tired out and overwhelmed, and it's easy to give up and simply float downstream again. We have to find a sustainable balance of effort. The skillful way of practice is not to force yourself to the center of the stream with an overexuberant effort. As anyone who has ever tried to swim upstream discovers, you can't go straight up the center of the current; you have to swim diagonally toward one side, then across toward the other, to make any progress. This requires a balance between effort and relaxation. Only a steady and relaxed effort will carry you upstream, against the current. It's that kind of steady and sustainable effort that allows addicts to make progress with their recovery.

As we bring awareness to our habits, tendencies, and world-views, we may see only how confused we have become. Sometimes all we can see is what we have lost, but eventually we come to know that we are safe again. We are now heading in the right direction, against the stream, against the old reactive tendencies and selfish pursuits. And although we long for quick progress, we can achieve nothing until we find the appropriately paced techniques.

The Buddha likened spiritual effort to the tuning of a stringed instrument. If the strings are too tight, it doesn't play correctly. If the strings are too loose, it doesn't sound right either. The path to recovery and freedom takes great effort and fine-tuning.

Here are some suggested guidelines for developing a recovery practice.

FROM THE BEGINNING

Start with the practice of meditation right away. Meditation is the most important tool in supporting your renunciation and beginning your recovery. Begin with the simple breath awareness concentration practice (see "Part 1: Breathing" on page 190). After a week or so of renunciation/abstinence, begin to alternate the Forgiveness Meditation on page 223 with breath practice every other day. Eventually we will want you to learn and practice all the meditations offered, but in the first few months of practice we encourage a focus on concentration and forgiveness.

TWO TO SIX MONTHS

Meditate for twenty minutes daily.

Go to as many meetings and meditation groups as you can.

Ask someone from the recovery community to mentor you and call him or her regularly to check in about your practice of the Four Truths.

Complete your First Truth Inventory and Second Truth Inventory.

Perform weekly physical practices like yoga, dance, or other exercises with mindfulness.

SIX TO TWELVE MONTHS

Increase your meditation practice to thirty minutes a day, and begin expanding the mindfulness practice to include forgiveness practice in your meditation for at least fifteen minutes every other day until you have no more resentments.

Attend a weekend retreat.

Begin making amends as part of the forgiveness process.

ONE TO FIVE YEARS

Begin daily meditation of forty-five minutes in one sitting or split into one thirty-minute and one fifteen-minute session.

After the first year of renunciation/sobriety/abstinence, begin practicing the four foundations of mindfulness and the heart practices of loving-kindness, compassion, appreciation, and equanimity.

Incorporate more and more mindfulness and heart practice in daily life.

Complete the amends process.

Attend a seven- to ten-day silent meditation retreat yearly.

After having completed a retreat and finished your amends, begin mentoring others.

Do an annual inventory on your recovery, looking at how you are currently engaging with the Four Truths and the Eightfold Path. Where are the weak links? What needs more attention and effort?

FIVE TO FIFTEEN YEARS

Stay involved, continue to practice, and share your experience, time, and energy with the newer people.

Include the forgiveness practice in your meditation for at least fifteen minutes every other day until you have no more resentments.

Try to attend a longer retreat that is one to three months in length.

Continue to do an annual inventory on your recovery, looking at how you are currently engaging with the Four Truths and the Eightfold Path. Where are the weak links? What needs more attention and effort?

FIFTEEN TO LIFE

Stay involved, continue to practice, and share your experience, time, and energy with the newer people.

Include the forgiveness practice in your meditation for at least fifteen minutes every other day, until you have no more resentments.

Continue the annual inventory on your recovery, looking at how you are currently engaging with the Four Truths and the Eightfold Path. Where are the weak links? What needs more attention and effort?

11

Mindfulness/Meditations

We develop wisdom through practicing formal mindfulness meditation. This leads to seeing clearly and
healing the root causes and conditions that lead to the
suffering of addiction. We practice present-time awareness in all aspects of our lives. We take refuge in the
present.

Mindfulness, or present-time awareness, is essential to finding
our way on the Eightfold Path. In fact, all the other factors of the
path depend on mindfulness of the present moment. Present-time
awareness is the experience of knowing what is happening as it
happens. Our recovery depends on us being present in mind as
well as in body. That is the only way to heal the wounds that led
to our addictions and to change our relationship to craving and the
repetitive habituations.

Mindfulness is defined as nonjudgmental, investigative, kind,
and responsive awareness. This sort of awareness takes intentional
training of the mind. Our attention is naturally scattered, the
mind constantly swinging from present, to future, to past, to
fantasy.

The Buddha referred to this tendency of our minds as the "monkey mind." Even for those of us who know that present-time awareness is the key to recovery, getting the attention to stay in the present is a difficult practice; we are trying to train the monkey. To be mindful of the present-time experiences of thoughts, feelings, sensations, and actions, we must vigilantly and continually redirect the attention to the here and now.

The formal training of mindfulness takes place in sitting meditation, through redirecting the attention or awareness to the breath, body, feeling tone, and process of mind, as well as the state of mind that has arisen. Yet life demands more than just paying attention during formal meditation periods. We must have the intention to be mindful and aware during *all* aspects of life.

FIRST FOUNDATION

The body is the best place to start. Through redirecting the attention from the thinking mind to the felt sense of the body, we begin to condition our attention to be in the here and now. This is done by returning our attention to the physical experience each time it wanders into thinking about the past or future.

The practice of mindfulness of the breath is especially helpful at the outset, because we are always breathing. Given that the breath always happens in the present moment, we know that if we are aware of the sensations of the breath, we have successfully brought our attention into the present moment. This first level of mindfulness offers us an experience of relaxation and allows us to start to let go of identification with the thinking aspect of our mind. By learning to ignore the thinking mind and pay attention to our bodies, we can successfully intervene on the cravings, doubts, fears, and other negative mind states that could lead to relapse.

(See the mindfulness of breathing instructions on page 190.)

But there is much more going on here to pay attention to than just the breath. So many sensations in our bodies, so many activities. The heart beating, internal organs processing food, skin sensations, bones, ligaments, saliva, blinking, eardrums being stimulated by sounds, eyes by images, noses by smell, tongues by taste. Our bodies are full of present-time information. What am I feeling, seeing, smelling, tasting, and thinking? Mindfulness is directed toward every aspect and activity of the body—posture, movement, emotion, everything.

We can focus on the four elements of our bodies through meditation, becoming aware of the heat, water, earth, and air within the process of our bodies.

(See the mindfulness of four elements instructions on page 197.)

In other meditations on the body, we may just focus on scanning our attention from the top of our heads to the bottom of our feet, to bring mindfulness to both the surface and internal parts of the body. We'll visualize the organs, muscles, and bones that create the body. (See the mindfulness of parts of the body instructions on page 195.)

As we pay close attention to our bodies, we begin to gain insight into the impermanent nature of all the phenomena of being, thoughts, feelings, and sensations arising and passing. We can also turn to a meditation on the impermanence of life in the body itself. We reflect on the inevitable death and decay of our bodies. Through death meditations we come to accept death and learn to cherish life.

The breath and the body are only the beginning of the mindfulness practice. Once we have established some level of present-time awareness and attention to the physical sensations of the body, we undertake training to bring attention to the feeling tone of the particular experience we are paying attention to.

SECOND FOUNDATION

Every single experience has a feeling tone to it—a quality of pleasantness, unpleasantness, or neutrality that we can perceive when
we are mindful. An awareness of the experience and its pleasant
or unpleasant tone is essential if we are to progress on the path
to recovery. Our habitual reaction to pleasurable experiences is to
cling to them, often falling into addictive patterns with pleasure.
Our habitual reaction to unpleasant experiences is to resist or push
them away. Clinging and aversion are the cause of most of the suffering we create for ourselves, and the roots of all addiction.

This second level of mindfulness, then, offers us awareness of
the causes of addictions. Through being mindful of the experience
and its feeling tone, we can directly examine our inner relationship
of clinging to pleasure and aversion to discomfort, which allows us
to respond to it deliberately, choosing to let go of the root cause of
what could become an addictive tendency or stressful suffering.

Without intentional mindfulness at this level of experience,
we have no choice but to stay stuck in the habits of aversion and
clinging. This keeps us locked into creating a miserable existence.
Paying careful attention to the present moment and our relationship with ourselves allows us to meet the unpleasant, the neutral,
and the pleasant with calm and understanding. At the heart of our
recovery is a simple choice: either we can stay addicted (clinging,
craving, and avoiding) and continue to suffer, or we can begin to
refrain from the substances, activities, and clinging (practicing
mindfulness and letting go) and find a deeper sense of well-being
and recover. (See the mindfulness of feeling tone instructions on
page 199.)

THIRD FOUNDATION

The third level of mindfulness brings attention to the process and contents of our mind. Having established present-time awareness of the body and feeling tone of experience, we then turn our mindfulness to the mind itself. This is done through paying close attention to our states of mind as they arise, including all the emotional experiences that are felt both mentally and physically. By paying close attention when the experiences of greed or anger are present, we begin to investigate what that state of mind feels like, where it arises from, where it goes, and how we relate to it.

This takes a level of intentional *nonreactivity:* we receive with awareness the state of mind and know it through direct experience, yet we allow it to arise and pass without trying to get rid of it or hold on to it. Rather than reacting with our usual attachment or aversion, taking everything personally and feeling the need to do something about it, we relax into the experience, seeing it clearly and simply letting it be, just as it is.

This is important on two levels. First, we become intimate with our mind states and with how they affect our mood and actions. Second, we begin to see more and more clearly that states of mind and emotions, like everything else, are impermanent. With mindfulness we have the choice of responding with compassion to the pain of craving, anger, fear, and confusion. Without mindfulness we are stuck in the reactive pattern and identification that will inevitably create more suffering and confusion.

This is certainly a radical practice, turning the attention toward the mind. It feels like a form of internal dissonance. We are rebelling against our mind's long-held habits. We are practicing internal discernment about what thoughts are wise and worthy of attention, and what thoughts are unwise and deserving of dismissal. This is one of the highest forms of recovery and inner freedom. No longer slaves to the dictates of the addict mind, we gain the ability to choose for ourselves how we respond to the thoughts, feelings, and sensations of being alive.

When we break free from a conditioned identification with the mind, we open a door to relating *to* our minds rather than *from* them. Then when your mind encourages you to drink, use, or engage in any of your addictive behaviors you can simply ignore it or respond directly to it by saying, "Nice try, mind, thanks for sharing."

(See the mindfulness of the mind instructions on page 201.)

FOURTH FOUNDATION

The fourth level of mindfulness is paying attention to the truth of the present-time experience—that is, paying attention to and knowing when suffering is present, when craving has arisen, and when contentment and peace are being experienced. This level of mindfulness extends to all the experiences we have, including the awareness of the arising and passing of the five hindrances of craving for pleasure, aversion to pain, restlessness, sloth, doubt; the six senses of hearing, seeing, smelling, tasting, thinking, and feeling; the Four Noble Truths of suffering, the cause, its end, and the path; and the seven factors of enlightenment, which are the experiences of mindfulness, investigation, tranquility, equanimity, patience, rapture, and concentration.

Through mindfulness we have insight into the attachments, clingings, and cravings that perpetuate our addictions. (See the mindfulness of the truth instructions on page 203.)

All these meditation instructions are applicable to any posture or movement of the body. Whether done walking, standing, sitting, or lying down, mindfulness and contemplative inquiry can and should be practiced. (See the mindfulness of walking instructions on page 204.)

Eventually all these meditations become one. The mindfulness of breath and body leads to the awareness of the feeling tone, then expands to the awareness of the content and process of the mind, and finally expands to include all the phenomena related to the mind/body process. This is the meditative training called the path of insight.

12

Concentration/Meditations

We develop the capacity to focus the mind on a single object, such as the breath or a phrase, training the mind through the practices of loving-kindness, compassion, and forgiveness to focus on the positive qualities we seek to uncover, and we utilize concentration at times of temptation or craving in order to abstain from acting unwisely.

Concentration, or focused attention, is another necessary tool on the path to recovery and freedom. When the mind is fully concentrated on one object—for example, on a mantra, a phrase, or a specific aspect of breath or body—you will often have a very pleasant, blissed-out experience. This is because when your mind is fully concentrated, you are no longer aware of the hindrances of sleepiness, restlessness, craving, doubt, and aversion. This can be a very useful experience in early recovery when the cravings are still very strong.

Concentration is developed by giving preference to a single object, such as the breath, a phrase or mantra, or any of the previous foundations of mindfulness. As we continually bring our attention back to the chosen object, the mind becomes more focused and able to see more clearly the nature of the chosen experience.

Our practice of mindfulness of breath is a concentration practice. Also when we practice forgiveness, loving-kindness, compassion, equanimity, and appreciation meditations, we repeat phrases over and over in our minds and this too concentrates the mind. These practices are also creating new thought patterns, new neural pathways.

(See the guided meditation instructions in the Heart Practices section on page 207.)

We honor and utilize concentration practices as an aspect of our path to recovery, but we also must issue a warning of caution. When the concentration wears off, the mind is still subject to those same difficult experiences. Thus the so-called spiritual experience of concentration meditations is really just the temporary phenomenon of bliss or nothingness. A temporary state of concentration can't change your relationship to the mind. It can't set you free from the confusion and difficulty in life; it only allows you to avoid or ignore it temporarily. Although the Buddha ultimately rejected concentration as the sole path to freedom, he realized that concentration was a useful tool, when integrated with mindfulness, to bring about insight and wisdom.

Concentration is best used to see the impermanent, impersonal, and unsatisfactory nature of all phenomena. These three insights— impermanence, impersonality, and unsatisfactoriness—are the keys to our recovery. Those who accept the world for how it is, rather than constantly wishing for something else, are on the path to freedom from addiction.

In times of craving and temptation, many have found it useful to replace the thoughts of acting out with a mantralike recitation of one of the Heart Practices, saying over and over, "May I be at ease" or "May I be free from suffering." This is a skillful way to redirect our attention and distract us from the craving that has arisen.

The level of concentration needed to fully benefit from the mindfulness/insight meditation practices is thought be in the area of being able sustain focus on the chosen object, the breath or phrase, for about ten minutes without getting lost in thought. Most people will be able to attain this level of concentration within a few months if they practice daily and diligently.

Concentration is one of our precious and useful tools on the path of recovery. If used wisely, it will profoundly help our process of awakening; if misused or abused, it could postpone our liberation indefinitely. Be wary of teachers or traditions that are only offering concentration-based practices. Mindfulness is the true cause of liberating insights; concentration supports mindfulness.

13

The Path to Heartfulness

As we walk the path of Refuge Recovery, we gradually uncover a loving heart. This is a process of awakening and healing that could be seen as analogous to an archaeological dig. In the early days, we remain on the surface. Mindfulness is our most important tool in the beginning, and it will give tremendous relief. It acts like a metal detector that allows us to know that there are precious treasures beneath the ground.

Mindfulness is also the shovel that begins the excavation. But as we begin to dig, we will likely first encounter all the layers of sediment that were covering the heart. The Heart Practices are a further refining of the soil. We may begin to sift through the rubble hoping to immediately find treasure.

But in the early days we may end up feeling more unsettled during compassion and kindness exercises because we are just uncovering all the skeletons that had been buried over the years of our addiction. We have probably become quite skilled at covering the insecurity and reactivity of our life, burying our hearts deeper and deeper. At the same time, each meditative effort of mindfulness, forgiveness, kindness, or compassion is another shovelful of dirt, each one getting us closer to the forgotten truth of our heart.

Perhaps, at times, the heart practices can be seen as even finer instruments of archaeology, like the brushes that are used to gently sweep away the remaining dust covering the treasure of our own heart. Meditations are versatile—sometimes you need a shovel doing the heavy lifting, and at other times you need something gentler, very subtle and refined, to simply dust off the heart.

But as we know, sometimes uncovering an ancient city can take a lifetime. There is no timetable that we can count on. There is no guarantee that we will reach the forgotten treasure of compassion anytime soon. What is promised is that it is there, waiting, and at times we can hear it calling to us, begging to be uncovered. The path of Refuge Recovery, if followed correctly and with persistence, will always lead to the recovery of our lost love and compassion, one scoop at a time.

We feel that it is only fair to also offer a warning. The path to uncovering our heart's positive qualities is a radical one. It is fraught with the demons of the heart/mind that in Buddhism we call *Mara*. Mara is the aspect of heart/mind that creates roadblocks, gives excuses, procrastinates, and urges us to avoid all the unpleasant mind states that accompany the healing of awakening. Mara is the inner experience of all forms of addiction, greed, hatred, and delusion. Mara will attack with vengeance at times, for by committing to the heart's liberation, we are committing to facing Mara directly.

The Buddha spoke of his battle with Mara, and victory over Mara was won with the weapons of love, compassion, equanimity, and appreciation. After the Buddha's initial victory, Mara did not give up, however. Mara continued to live with the Buddha throughout his whole life. The Buddha was constantly vigilant, always meeting Mara with a loving awareness, always disarming him with the heart's wisest responses. We too can live a life of responding wisely to Mara, to our addictive patterns, to the pain of our past.

Everyone has the ability to recover, love, forgive, and be compassionate. Ability is our birthright. The only issues are desire and willingness. Most people would readily confess the desire to be free from the addictions, hatred, anger, and fear that they live with, although there are those of us who have been so badly injured and confused that they have lost all hope. Some of us have even created a belief in hatred as a noble and necessary quality. Our experience shows us that even the most deeply wounded and confused hearts are healed when the principles outlined in our program of recovery are applied.

We welcome you to the Refuge Recovery way. If you follow this path, you will free yourself from all the unnecessary suffering of addiction, and you will inspire others to do the same. The practices in this book are not a quick fix; they are a map to a hidden treasure. You will have to do all the digging yourself, hopefully with the support of teachers and community, but it is ultimately up to you to do the heavy lifting, or letting go as it may be. Your life will transform, as ours have, and together we will create a positive change in this world.

14

Breaking the Addiction

One of the problems we face as addicts is that we get comfortable. Even though we don't always like the reality of our situation, it becomes familiar. We don't like the dissatisfaction, the suffering, and the difficulty of life. We wish it were different, but we are so comfortable in it. It is all we have ever known.

Like a child who is abused by his or her parents—a child who screams for the familiar "comfort" of those parents as they're being hauled off by the police for beating the child to a pulp—we would rather stay with the familiar than face the unknown, even when what's familiar is our suffering. We are so used to our confusion that when the choice for freedom comes, we think, *No way—it's too hard.* Because the unknown is too scary, we go through our lives repeating patterns of thought and action even when they bring us pain.

We also sometimes get lost in delusional philosophies that explain the difficulties of life. We like such philosophies because, being scared, we feel we have to have the right answer all the time. Many of the world's religious traditions are a direct reaction to the confusion and difficulty of life. It is difficult to rest in not knowing, so we create the delusion of knowledge. Humans devise creation myths, psychological theories, cultural norms, political beliefs, and religions, all in a vain attempt to appease or control their core feelings of insecurity and uncertainty. What Buddhism offers that differs from most other theories is a direct experience of what is true. Buddhism doesn't ask for blind faith or belief; it offers a practical path to walk. We cannot find freedom by thinking about it with an untrained mind. The untrained mind is not trustworthy; it is filled with greed, hatred, and delusion. Only the mind trained in mindfulness, friendliness, and investigation can directly experience the freedom from suffering that will satisfy the natural longing for security. This is the wisdom of insecurity.

We can often see the manifestation of this fear of the unknown in relationships. We go through our lives attached to our familiar suffering by getting into the same type of unsatisfactory relationships again and again. How many times do we have to fall in love with someone just like Mommy or Daddy before we acknowledge the pattern of seeking love as an attempt to heal an old wound? Does it ever really work? With mindful investigation, we can see for ourselves what our patterns and habitual reactions are—and from that place of true knowledge, we can then begin to choose our responses, actions, and partners more wisely.

Life doesn't have to be so unsatisfactory. This is the good news: there is a cause to our confusion and suffering—it is our relationship to craving—and that cause can be altered to bring about a different effect. Notice that here, we don't say it's craving itself that's the problem. That's just a natural phenomenon of the conditioned heart-mind. No, the problem lies in our *addiction* to satisfying the craving. We all experience craving. When we have a pleasant experience, we crave more of it—we wish for it to increase or at least to last. When we have an unpleasant experience, we crave for it to go away. We feel the need to escape from pain, to destroy it and to replace it with pleasure. This is especially true for the addict, who has set in motion a long-term habitual reaction of avoiding pain and creating pleasure with substances or behaviors he or she became addicted to.

We are addicted to pleasure, in part because we confuse pleasure with happiness. We would all say that deep down, all we want is to be happy. Yet we don't have a realistic understanding of what happiness really is. Happiness is closer to the experience of acceptance and contentment than it is to pleasure. True happiness exists as the spacious and compassionate heart's willingness to feel whatever is present.

Though pleasure is in no way the enemy in our search for happiness, it comes and goes. When it's here, we tend to grasp at it; when it's gone, we want more. That addiction is the untrained heart-mind's natural reaction to anything pleasurable. This is clear in the Buddha's Second Noble Truth: the cause of suffering is craving for pleasure.

Though we speak of ourselves as addicts, drug addicts, sex addicts, alcoholics, food addicts, what we are really addicted to isn't the substances or the behaviors—drugs or sex or food or alcohol—but our own minds. We are addicted to that part of the mind that craves, that says we must satisfy this desire or that. Even in 12-step recovery programs that view addiction as a disease, it is said that the drugs and alcohol are only a symptom of an internal imbalance. That's why we say that our *relationship* to craving is the problem, not the substances or behaviors themselves.

We have all paid the price for that unwise relationship to craving. Most of the suffering in life is due to our addiction to our thoughts and cravings. We wander through life constantly craving more of the pleasant stuff and less of the unpleasant. This is the place where the spiritual practice of recovery comes in. The Buddha's "against the stream" principle tells us that it's counterinstinctual: it goes against our very human survival instincts to accept pain and not chase pleasure. It is a veritable internal battle, because breaking the addiction to our knee-jerk satisfaction of craving goes against our natural human tendencies. When life is uncomfortable, we naturally want it to change; when life is good, we want things to stay as they are. It goes against our nature to stop trying to satisfy our craving, to allow the craving to be there without reacting to it.

Few of us have the courage to accept pain as pain and pleasure as pleasure, and to find the place of peace and serenity that accepts both pain and pleasure as impermanent and ultimately impersonal. But our confusion may also go beyond the courage to train the mind.

Other than Buddhism, few teachings even allow for the possibility of this kind of freedom. Most of us have a fantasy of spiritual awakening as being purely pleasurable all the time. This fits right in with our craving for pleasure, but also with the creation of more suffering. The awakening of the Buddha within each one of us is the experience of nonsuffering. Not suffering could be considered blissful in comparison to suffering, but that does not mean that it is pleasurable all the time. We have to let go of our fantasy of unending pleasure and the craving for a pain-free existence. That is not the kind of spiritual awakening that the Buddhist path of recovery offers.

The important question, then, is, How do we break this addiction? How do we loosen our identification with craving and the satisfying of our desires? How do we break our addiction to our minds? How do we get free?

The untrained mind, the natural state of human consciousness, has very little free will. We talk about free will, about freedom of choice, but without training the mind, we don't truly have the ability to choose. We are actually slaves to, or addicted to, the dictates of the past, of our conditioning—of our karma, or past actions. We don't have free will unless we bring mindful awareness to the moment-to-moment process of craving arising. The short version of this principle is that we have the ability to break our habitual addictive reactions through close attention to the mind and body.

The foundational practice is paying attention to our mind, our body, and our present-time experience. It is hard to pay attention, because we have to face some ugly truths and tolerate some discomfort. One ugly truth may be that our fear, lust, or anger is all we see in the beginning. Since the mind does not easily pay attention to the present, effort is necessary. The mind, which is all over the place from one moment to the next, has to be trained. The Buddha said the mind was like a monkey swinging in a tree from one branch to the next. Yes, that is what the mind does: it swings from one thought to the next, from the future to the past, from planning to remembering, from self-hatred to grandiosity. To get some stability, we need the intentional effort of repeatedly bringing the attention back, of paying attention to the present-time experience of breath and body, over and over.

In fact, we are paying attention to *something* all the time, though it may be a fantasy in our mind, perhaps a daydream about a more pleasant future. Through redirecting our attention to the present moment, to the simple reality of our breath and body, and through investigating the feeling tone of each experience, we open ourselves to the possibility of freedom.

Right now there is the experience of sitting here reading this book. Is it pleasant or unpleasant? Are you meeting the sensations in your body with aversion or compassion?

Bringing awareness to the feeling tone in this moment allows us to relax and release the aversion. Our habitual tendency, when there is discomfort, is to push it away, but the aversion to that discomfort seems to make it grow bigger, and pretty soon we begin squirming around or we feel that we have to run out of the room because sitting still is a pain in the ass.

Awareness of the desire for things to be other than the way they are is key. Thus the first step in breaking the addiction is acknowledging the unsatisfactory nature of both pleasure and pain. We do this by being vigilant toward and aware of the presence of dissatisfaction, the desire for things to be different. Yet we also need to pay attention to moments of ease and well-being, the experience of nonattachment, when the mind is free from suffering. We are usually hypervigilant when something is uncomfortable, yet when it is pleasurable or peaceful, we often pay no attention, except perhaps to think about how we are going to get more of that pleasure.

Awareness of the lack of satisfaction and of the craving for things to be different allows us to take the next step toward freedom. We can relax the clinging of the mind and body and simply accept that we feel a craving for more or less of something. We can ask ourselves, *Can I accept this one moment at a time? Can I acknowledge that this is the way it is, and though I want things to be different, can I let go of that aversion and let things be the way they are?*

It is important to acknowledge this process as it unfolds by investigating it and acknowledging our feelings of craving. Our conditioned tendency is to push or pull or grasp or run. The practice of Refuge Recovery calls us to the practice of letting go or letting be. From the awareness of grasping or aversion comes the possibility of letting go. With the trained mind, we can release our mental or physical grip. Because all things that have arisen will pass, that act of letting go will allow the experience to pass. Letting be is similar to letting go: it means letting the experience (and all the feelings it engenders) be present the way that it is, accepting the experience as unsatisfactory, impermanent, and impersonal.

In the early stages of recovery, we may find that we are not so good at internally just letting things go or letting ourselves be, but with time we will become able to tolerate unpleasantness without externalizing it and acting on it. For example, we won't have to say the angry words; we may still experience the anger or fear, but we gain the ability to pause and respond with compassion rather than react with angst.

The Buddha suggests that once we have acknowledged our clinging or aversion, if we can't easily let it go, we should try redirecting our attention to something else, to another place in the body that is not painful. For example, during meditation if there is pain in your left knee and you feel the aversion to it but can't accept or tolerate it, redirect your attention somewhere else; try, for example, bringing the attention back to the breath.

Another level of our practice that addresses craving is inquiry. We can investigate what is going on. What is underneath this desire, more or less? What is motivating or fueling this aversion? Why is this thought pattern being played over and over again? When we really start to investigate our aversion, anger, or lust, we almost always find that what is fueling it underneath is fear—a base-level fear that we are not going to get what we want or are going to lose what we have. Sometimes it even manifests as a fear that we won't be able to tolerate the fear.

Underneath our ego and anger and lust is often the insecurity of fear, which we find when we investigate. Once we recognize it as fear, we can reflect on the fact that fear is not an excuse for inaction. We can then take the next breath or other action and learn to live with fear as a constant companion. If we lived our lives taking action only when fear was not at play, we would do very little. We certainly never would have started meditating in the first place. Almost every time we do something new some fear arises, but it is not a problem, just an old and familiar companion. In fact, for recovering addicts, the wisdom of insecurity becomes one of our greatest teachers.

Another level of inquiry is to look closely at our mind to see who is experiencing this fear. *Whose fear is this? Is it mine?* Sometimes it becomes clear that the voices of fear are not even our own.

We are hearing our parents, teachers, friends, or enemies. We have incorporated those voices into our psyche and have believed them our whole life, thinking that the feelings and thoughts of fear were somehow personal.

On a deeper level, we investigate who is really experiencing all this craving. It's really just the mind, isn't it? Just more impermanent thoughts arising and passing.

If neither letting go nor investigating works, another skillful way to address craving is to attempt to replace it by actively reflecting on love, courage, and kindness. Since negative mind states are still just mind states, we can try to replace them with positive mind states. The loving-kindness meditation practice (see the example on page 214) is designed for this.

Becoming aware of what we are addicted to and becoming committed to getting free from our misidentification with and addiction to our minds, thoughts, and feelings require a level of renunciation—a level of being honest with ourselves and realizing that we keep doing the same thing over and over, and the outcome is unsatisfactory every time. Part of our work in recovery is to break the denial of believing that things are going to be different this time. And then beginning to change our inner and outer actions.

Here is a simple story that points to the process by which these changes are often made. It takes place in five phases or chapters:

1. We are walking down the street and we fall down a hole. We don't know what happened, and it takes us a long time to get out of that hole.

2. The next time we walk down the same street, we know that there is a hole there but we are still attracted to it, and we get curious and we fall in again, but this time it takes us less time to get out.

3. The next time we walk down the same street, we know that there is a hole there but we are pretty sure we can jump over it, and we try to jump over but fall in again.

4. The next time we walk down the same street, we know the danger but are still curious, so we walk up to the hole and look in, thinking, *Damn, that's a deep hole,* but this time we don't fall into it; this time we carefully walk around it.

5. Finally, we choose to walk down a different street, deciding that we won't walk down that old street anymore because we know there's a hole there!

On the path of recovery, we need to have that fifth level of renunciation—a commitment that we are not going to walk down the streets of intoxication and indulgence anymore. Of course it isn't so simple—our habits and grasping are so deep—but it all starts with the intention to change, to find new ways of relating to our mind.

All this points toward breaking the addiction to pleasure and the aversion to pain. We each have to ask ourselves, *What do I really want in my life, short-term satisfaction of craving or long-term peace of mind and the healing of the heart that will lead to a full recovery of my true nature?*

When we choose the path of wanting long-term peace, freedom, and true happiness in our lives rather than the short-term satisfaction of pleasure and desire, then the effort to train the mind is there. This has been our experience. When we really keep in the forefront of our thoughts that our intention in this life is to recover and be free, then being of service, practicing meditation, and doing what we need to do to get free becomes the only rational decision.

This takes discipline, effort, and a deep commitment. It takes a form of rebellion, both inwardly and outwardly, because we not only subvert our own conditioning, we also walk a path that is to-tally countercultural. The status quo in our world is to be attached to pleasure and to avoid all unpleasant experiences. Our path leads upstream, against the normal human confusions and sufferings.

The commitment to this path of recovery will take stamina. Steadfastness and perseverance are a necessity if we are to continue on a long-term spiritual path. We wish we could say that there's some magical secret to all this—that *this* or *that* is what it takes to persevere, but we have no easy solution.

Perhaps it is as simple as courage—the courage to begin, to continue, and to complete the task we took birth for. Yet fear is, has been, and perhaps always will be our constant companion on this path of recovery. Courage is not the absence of fear; it is the willingness to act in spite of being afraid.

Freeing yourself from the addiction to your mind is like going off into the wilderness to a place you've never been before. It makes perfect sense that we want to stay attached to our suffering because it is so familiar. What we most fear is not darkness—we know the darkness all too well; what we are most afraid of is the light. The light of freedom shines from the unknown, undiscovered truths of compassion, kindness, appreciation, forgiveness, and the wisdom to respond with care and understanding to all beings.

But like any arduous journey that feels like it will never end, the path of recovery has both rewards and a destination. Along the way, as we face our fears and confusion, we begin to realize that the process is perfectly safe and well worth the effort to persevere. The closer we get, the less scary it becomes. And when we make it through the dense forests, we can enjoy the views from a higher elevation on the path.

PART TWO

Reflections on Recovery

The following are personal recovery stories from members of our Refuge Recovery community. We have included these stories for those new to recovery to get a sense of the various ways in which recovery happens. You are not alone in your suffering, your confusion, or your path of healing and recovery.

15

Lynne

I grew up in Berkeley, California, in the 1950s. I began drinking when I was in high school. I drank because I wanted to fit in with my peers. After graduation, I went away to college but left after a semester and got married because I was pregnant. At the time, my drinking was limited to weekends, socializing with my husband and our friends. I didn't start drinking every day until a few years later, when my husband and I split up. I started to drink every night after work, which seemed perfectly normal, having grown up in a home where my parents drank every evening. But I had a low tolerance for alcohol and often found myself in compromising situations. I experimented with various types of drugs as well, which were prevalent during the '60s. I behaved in ways I never would have behaved sober, and I did things that were not in my daughter's best interest.

On one occasion, I was living in Santa Barbara as part of a communal living situation. My drinking eventually got me kicked out. In need of a place to stay, I bought a tent and lived in it with my four-year-old daughter for three weeks. A year or so later, I returned to Northern California, began working as a mail carrier, and met my second husband. After seven years of marriage, we divorced and I moved again. One night after a party, I got pulled over for drunk driving and was taken to jail in handcuffs. Although I found this experience humiliating, it did not stop my drinking. I remember the look of disgust on my daughter's face each time I walked in the house drunk or brought my date home for the night. I continued drinking and using drugs for many years. It wasn't until after my daughter graduated from college when I hit bottom.

In 1984, my daughter married, my father died, I took a trip to Europe, and I got clean and sober. My sobriety date is November 25. I woke up the Friday after Thanksgiving with a hangover. There was nothing unusual about my drinking the day before; nothing dramatic had happened. It was just another day of misery. What was different was that I talked about it in a counseling session later that day. I admitted to the therapist that I drank too much and took Valium. Her response surprised me. She told me that if I wanted to continue seeing her, I would have to go to Alcoholics Anonymous (AA). I had tried for over a year to stop drinking on my own and had been unsuccessful. My solutions had not worked, and my outlook on life was bleak. At home, after the counseling appointment, I phoned someone I knew who went to AA and asked him where I could find a meeting. He offered to come to my house and talk to me. During our talk he told me his story of finding recovery and then directed me to a meeting that night.

I drove to the meeting with trepidation. When I arrived, I debated about whether or not to go inside. I could not believe that my life had come to this. I was furious that I had to walk into a room and sit down with a group of people who I imagined were losers. I don't remember much of what was said at that meeting, but I do remember that when the meeting was over, I was surrounded by women giving me phone numbers and talking about a Big Book. They told me to come back the next day at noon. My head was swimming; they all seemed overly friendly and much too excited. What did I have in common with these women? Did I even belong in AA? The whole thing seemed so corny, saying "Hi, so and so," and having placards on the wall with sayings that were so elementary. Nevertheless, I began going to AA meetings every day and received a twenty-four-hour chip. I enjoyed the attention paid to me as a newcomer. I was still a reluctant participant, however.

I surrendered to the program of AA a week later. It was a Monday night. I recall the moment vividly. I arrived just before the meeting started and sat in the back of the room. I was feeling defeated. A woman in front of me turned around and said hello. She asked me what time of day was most difficult for me. I told her it was when I got home from work. She gave me her phone number and told me to call her every day when I got home. That was the beginning of my journey in Alcoholics Anonymous, and she was my first sponsor.

Making the decision to participate in AA was a pivotal point in my life because I chose to go down an unfamiliar path. I adopted a new way of life in order to save my life. I trusted that a group of people in AA knew better than I did how to live sober. I turned my life and will over to the group. That was my third step—Made a decision to turn our will and our life over to the care of God as we understood him—because I did not believe in God. Turning my life over to the group worked because I am sober today. However, I made a sacrifice that I was unaware of at the time. I gave up self-reliance. In order to fit in and to be part of the AA group, I believed that I could no longer rely on myself. The AA literature states that we must rely on a Higher Power in order to stay sober. More would be revealed.

In 1988, with four years of sobriety, I attended a workshop on living and dying led by Stephen Levine. He offered to teach medi-

tation to anyone who was interested, so a group of us met at seven
A.M. before the workshop began. I was thus introduced to Vipassana meditation. I began practicing and noticed the benefits immediately. I had spent five years doing transcendental meditation
in the 1970s so I had faith in the benefit of a meditation practice.

With daily meditation I found myself feeling calmer and more
focused. I noticed a shift in the way I responded to difficult situations. More important, I felt connected in a way I had never felt
before. When I listened to AA members talk about feeling connected to their Higher Power, I could not relate. Nor did I relate
when members said that coming to AA was like coming home. For
me, finding meditation was like coming home.

So began a regular meditation practice. Some days I meditated
for five minutes and other days for twenty minutes. I began attending daylong retreats at Spirit Rock Meditation Center in Marin
County and reading books on mindfulness, meditation, and Buddhism. I was dedicated to the practice of meditation, yet I felt like
I was living in two worlds. No one I knew in AA was interested
in Buddhism or formal meditation practice. Meditation was mentioned in AA's eleventh step; however, it was closely connected
with the Prayer of St. Francis. I did not feel comfortable talking
about meditation with my friends in AA, nor did I feel comfortable
talking about my recovery with people I encountered in meditation
circles.

What became clear to me is that I felt ashamed of being an
alcoholic. Being a meditator definitely held a higher status in my
mind. My feelings associated with alcoholism were not unfounded.
As a social worker, I met plenty of professionals who expressed
negative views of those with drug or alcohol problems.

For years I went to meetings, worked the steps with a sponsor,
and walked the AA talk. I also had a meditation practice. At times
I felt like immersing myself in a Buddhist way of life. Then guilt

would set in and I would remember that I was an alcoholic, which meant that I was bound to the program. I had heard it said over and over again in AA meetings that if I did not follow the AA program of recovery, I would drink again. It felt like I had no choice when it came to AA.

In 1992, I attended my first residential meditation retreat, a six-day women's retreat. In a student/teacher interview, I identified myself as an alcoholic. Looking back, I realize that with seven years of sobriety I saw myself first and foremost as an alcoholic. My sobriety had not yet given me a sense of who I was without that label.

In the summer of 1995, I hit a wall. I was doing everything the program suggested, but my life felt empty. I was depressed and lacking spirit. With over ten years of sobriety I knew what the AA solution would be: rework the steps and work with others. Another option, quoted in the Big Book, is to seek outside help, which is what I did.

With some encouragement, I made the decision to attend a weeklong outpatient workshop called Survivors offered by an addictions treatment center in Arizona. The workshop delves into childhood trauma that impacts current-day life. It involved five days of intense experiential work based on past events in my life that were traumatic. The resulting emotions were processed with the goal of resolving any remaining grief. Although I had discussed childhood issues over the years in counseling, at this point in my sobriety I was interested in digging deeper in order to resolve those issues. I flew from California to Arizona and checked in for the workshop, which involved daily group work and lots of writing. A small group of us met each day with two well-trained facilitators. On the last day of the workshop, I told one of the leaders that I felt ripped open and unable to put myself back together. She suggested I become an inpatient in the treatment center. I spent the next five weeks in treatment where I was forced to look at some painful, unresolved issues from my past.

In the process, I uncovered beliefs that were blocking my progress in recovery. The primary belief I discovered was that I felt unworthy of love. The underlying message I gave myself was "something is wrong with me." A belief related to that was that I needed to be perfect in order to be loved.

Returning home, I resumed my AA way of life, yet something about me was different. The time in Arizona sparked something in me, and I had started to question what was said in AA meetings. A shift had taken place; I had befriended myself.

Another important shift occurred in my life at this time. After twenty-two years of being single, I met a man who would become my husband. For the next five years, my primary focus was on developing a healthy relationship with him. Although I had been married before, this marriage felt like a first. The fact that we were both in recovery and brought a willingness to be present for the relationship made a huge difference. This was also a time of transition. We moved from the Bay Area in California to Bend, Oregon, and started life together in a new community. As we became connected to the AA community in Bend, we also became aware of a shared interest in meditation. I continued my meditation practice, and my husband began to join me in that practice.

In 2000, we helped start a meditation Sangha in Bend. A year later we returned to California for three years to finish earning retirement credits. During that time, we attended a weekly Sangha with an established teacher and had the opportunity to attend one-day retreats. As a result, we expanded our knowledge of Vipassana meditation and Buddhism. For the three years we lived in California we were also part of the AA and Al-Anon communities. About this same time I began attending meditation retreats once a year.

After returning to Oregon in 2004, I attended a weekend retreat with Noah Levine. I was attracted to his retreat because it encouraged social workers to attend and referred to the Buddhist path as revolutionary. In my heart I am a revolutionary, and I was excited at the prospect of viewing the Buddhist path in this way. In addition, I had been to several workshops with Noah's father, Stephen Levine, in the 1970s and 1980s and had a great deal of respect for his teachings.

The weekend experience was invigorating for me, lending a new view to the incorporation of Buddhist thought into my recovery life. Although the retreat topic was not related to 12-step recovery, many people there were in recovery and Noah made references to his recovery. It was a comfortable atmosphere for me.

Fast-forward to 2010. By then, I had attended two seven-day meditation retreats that I found to be very beneficial to my meditation practice. A major turning point for me came in September 2010, when Noah led a two-day retreat titled "Breaking the Addiction to Our Minds: A Buddhism and Recovery Retreat." Five of us from Bend AA, including my husband, attended this retreat. It was a pivotal point on my recovery path. Over the course of the weekend I had numerous insights related to my recovery in AA and was free to speak about AA and Buddhism in the same room. The retreat provided a forum for all of us, in or out of AA, to talk about our struggles with addiction and to find solutions in the Buddhist path. Noah told us about the Buddhist recovery groups meeting in Los Angeles twice a week. He shared with us his meeting format including the Four Truths of Recovery, the Eightfold Path to Recovery, and A Buddhist Version of the 12 Steps. With these in hand, the five of us from Bend returned home and started a Buddhist recovery group.

Connecting the dots. In Noah's preamble, he states: "All beings have the power and potential to free themselves from suffering." This statement was an *aha* moment for me. Earlier I said that I gave up self-reliance. I understand now why I was stuck for so many years. I did not trust myself. In AA I had been taught to rely on a power outside myself and I took that instruction literally.

In his Eightfold Path to Recovery, Noah states: " . . . We believe in the human capacity for change." That means that I not only have the capacity for change, but that I can rely on myself to seek that change. When I befriended myself, at ten years sober, I began seeking answers from within. In doing so, I regained self-reliance. Without self-reliance, how could I trust that following the Buddhist path would keep me on the path? And without trust in myself, how could I follow a path (Buddhism) that tells me to trust in my own experience?

In the third of the Four Truths of Recovery, Noah states: " . . . eventually you will come to a verified faith in the path of recovery/awakening through the actions you take on the path."

Although it took me years to bring AA recovery and Buddhism together, it was through my personal experiences in both AA and Buddhist recovery that I was able to do so. The pieces of the puzzle now fit. With trust in myself, and the teachings to guide me, I can navigate the path.

16

Jordan

As I walked down the alley near my mother's house, I noticed a feeling of confidence that I hadn't felt in years. I was oddly aware that the sense of pride was because I was the one holding the pot. I felt wanted and it felt great. My friends watched with anticipation as I loaded the pipe and took the first hit. The warm smoke filled my lungs and exploded out, leaving me coughing as I'd never coughed before. A feeling of gushy happiness filled my body as I closed my eyes and thanked the universe for showing me this magical plant, and, at that very moment, I vowed to do whatever necessary to feel this way for the rest of my life.

My earliest memories are happy. My parents showered me with love, attention, and affection. They had suffered through three miscarriages and were told they would never conceive, so when I was born, I inherited all the yearning and longing they had in their hearts. Not to imply that this would discount the infinite love and joy they would have for the two miracle pregnancies to come.

I think I might have been the happiest little boy in the history of little boys. I would spend hours crawling on my mother's bed, curling under the covers as she read me a book. At four years old, I was given a daily afternoon bath, courtesy of my paternal grandmother who came to stay at my house and help babysit me while my mother was on bed rest for the last four months of her second pregnancy. The water was always the perfect temperature—not too hot and not too cold—as I held tiny plastic model airplanes and swirled them through the air and then turned them into submarines. I'm told that, around that time, I was very curious about God and mesmerized by the idea that my mom's big fat belly had a person in it. It was not uncommon for me to exclaim, "Geez, isn't God so great!" then ask "Why does God make some people homeless?"

Elementary school would prove to instill more questions. It was during that time when I first noticed that I didn't have control over my body. This body, the one I thought I could control, would rule me. At times it would twitch or jerk. Sometimes it would expel strange noises from my mouth. These movements were involuntary. Like a sneeze, I couldn't help it. I was soon diagnosed with Tourette syndrome, a neurological disorder that makes the brain misfire and send random motor and vocal impulses.

The kids at my small school were kind enough not to laugh in my face when I would suddenly jerk my neck to the side or randomly let out a little yelp. They did their best to hide their jokes, but I always knew. I felt like embarrassment incarnate. I was convinced I was broken, that I was inherently defective.

It was around this time, at ten or eleven years old, that I had my first drink. A school friend's parents were throwing a big party at their house, and we kids were allowed to set up a tent and spend the night having an adventure in the backyard. Looking around, I saw three distinct cliques—the adults, the older kids, and me and my friends. I couldn't have cared less about the adults and I loved my friends, but there was something about those older kids. They all seemed like they were in the midst of the best night of their lives. A few of them were even smoking cigarettes . . . I thought only adults were allowed to do that.

A couple hours into the night, one of my friends said we should go try a sip of alcohol. I had remembered that my dad would sometimes pour a few different liquids into the same glass when he drank alcohol. So, naturally, we poured a little bit of whatever kind of booze there was around the bar into an empty aluminum can of Coke. Back in the tent, we each took turns taking a swig of the concoction—the most vile mixture of gin, rum, red wine, beer, and vodka. We all had that same initial reaction. Our faces cringed as we trembled with disgust. But, pushing past the wretched taste and sensation of my throat being on fire, I knew I had just experienced a sliver of something great. Unlike the others, I drank as much of that gross firewater as I could before throwing up and surrendering to bed.

With puberty in full swing, middle school was not particularly fun. Social status was a new and difficult concept. I suddenly had to impress girls. And that was all on top of being the kid in the back of the classroom who, during exam time, would spontaneously rupture silence with noises that could have been ejected from Chewbacca's very mouth. My self-esteem took a beating with every tick I tocked. And though I had a good group of friends, some of whom I'm thankfully still close with, I would have done anything to crawl into a hole and never come out.

By twelve, this feeling of isolation, which had previously been confined to school grounds, had started to spread. I began to feel lonely at home as well. My father had recently landed the job of his dreams, which unfortunately took up more and more of his time. The lack of his presence at home became impossible to ignore. Even when he was home, it seemed like he was on his phone the majority of the time. I came to the conclusion that if I were important to my father, he'd act differently.

That walk down the alley with pot, my newly discovered savior, couldn't have come at a better time. I honored the vow I made, got high at every opportunity, and became very skilled at creating an abundance of those opportunities. No one on earth could tell me to put down this thing that turned my bad feelings into good ones. I now had a sense of identity and interminable access to a vacation I had so hungered for—time off from the turmoil going on at home and, most important, a break from my mind.

And God knows I'd need it for the random Wednesday evening my parents sat my brothers and me down saying they had something they wanted to talk to us about. Sensing something ominous was about to present itself, I sat down with a knot in my throat. It was clear they were nervous too, which only exacerbated my fear. They told us that they were getting a divorce and that my dad was moving out.

At some point in the conversation there was mention of God. "He has a plan for everyone," someone said, "so there's no need to worry." That felt like the ultimate betrayal—that there's a plan and everything's going to turn out all right. Why, when something bad happens, am I told God works in mysterious ways? How can people be so stupid to mistake meanness for mystery? I sat there listening to the two people whom I once viewed as all-knowing, perfect beings. I still can't find the words to fully express the mixture of sadness, anger, betrayal, and disillusion I felt. It was as if everything I'd ever been told was a complete and utter lie. There were no happy endings. There was no happily ever after.

Shortly after my dad moved out I had my first blackout. My dad took my brothers and me to our cousins' house for dinner. I was pestering my dad to let me taste the wine that he and the other adults were drinking. He inevitably caved and poured a tiny splash into a cup. After that, I have a fuzzy memory of sneaking into the basement of my cousins' house to steal a bottle of wine. That's where my recollection of that night ends.

I woke up the next day very late in the afternoon with a massive headache, which I thought was very odd. I yelled out for my cousin James who was supposed to have spent the night. James was nowhere to be found. Instead, my dad appeared with a look of immense fear. I asked where James was. "Don't you remember the long talk we had?" my dad responded. "Because you were acting out and insulting me, you lost the privilege to have James sleep over."

I sat still, racking my brain, so confused as to why I had absolutely no clue about the intense encounter that my dad had recounted—I must have looked like a deer in the headlights. With comedic timing, I lunged forward and threw up.

The parallel timing of my declining personal life and my launch into drugs and alcohol was never lost to me. Whether I was willing to openly admit this or not, I knew my using was a symptom of deep emotional and spiritual wounds and confusion. I concluded that the heartbreak of caring was too much and, if I never invested in another or let anyone else in close enough, I would be safe. It became instinctual for me to distance myself from anyone or anything I thought could break my heart. This philosophy turned out to only create feelings of loneliness, futility, and a core belief that I was unworthy.

My using quickly progressed, and I became more and more apathetic toward the world. What might be considered "social using" was over. I would always observe other people's attitudes toward getting high and, without exception, acknowledge that I had a different relationship to drugs and alcohol. I wanted and needed them. I was on the edge and about to jump into the self-imposed prison of hopelessness. My grades dropped lower than they had ever been, and I was soon kicked out of my first high school when the principal came across the little bong I kept in my locker.

Drained from dealing with the turmoil in their lives, my parents were easy prey. I had become an expert in knowing what heartstrings to pull and when. Getting kicked out of school was a surprisingly painless ordeal. I didn't even get grounded. My parents wanted so badly to trust me. It's amazing what people will believe based on their desire for it to be true. You find what you look for.

My new school was a haven for getting high. I ran into friends whom I knew from parties. The atmosphere reminded me of a burglar going back to jail and reuniting with all his burglar friends. These guys were just like me. We were the people at the party whose sole mission was to drink as much as we could and get as high as possible. The day I started the new school I took a few Vicodins. By now, this was very normal, if not necessary—I was a miserable person to be around if I didn't get something in my system each morning. That day during lunch, these friends took me to an abandoned school bus where we smoked pot, watching the teachers and students walk across campus. In the same way two gifted athletes competing against each other will raise the level of play, these friends and I pushed each other to new levels of consumption.

I tried to do well in school. I was a great starter. I would begin a project or start "a new chapter in my life" with very real intentions of straightening up my act. It was always "different this time." And I sincerely cared. The problem was that I had lost all tolerance of discomfort. The moment a feeling or thought that wasn't wanted crept in, I was off, chasing a high. Life was either running to drugs or running away from pain. It was a constant battle to "keep it together." When I enjoyed getting high, I couldn't control it. When I tried to control getting high, I couldn't enjoy it.

In hopes of getting me sober, my parents sent me to a therapist who introduced me to meditation. I took to meditation from the start. The concentration practice I was taught provided me with a sense of calm reminiscent of the first time I got high. But the feeling never stayed too long, and there was no way meditation was going to be able to compete with my active addiction.

I wanted my mom not to worry about me so much. Yet time and again I would claim change only to disappoint. Rather than engage in arguments and yell, my mother carried the faint air of surrender in the face of my bullshit. Rather than raise her voice, she would simply say, "I'm disappointed in you." The sadness in her eyes when she looked at me was unbearable. I put on the mask of anger and puffed my chest to tell the world I didn't care, but that was a lie. I just could not deal with how overwhelming caring could be.

There were certain drugs that I saw as "the bad drugs" that I never let my circle of friends know I used. I did them either with my dealer or by myself. Even though my close friends were doing a lot of these drugs, I had such a deluded, shame-filled perception that I thought if they saw me using those drugs, they would think I was scum. It was self-obsession and egocentricity to epic proportions. I was the piece of shit that the world revolved around. It's comical that I hated myself so much when all I thought about and cared about was me.

The last year of my drinking and drugging was a downward spiral. I lived in a constant state of desperation. I had to drink; it was no longer a choice, nor was it fun. The pleasant feelings of confidence and escape that I experienced in the beginning of my using were long gone. I did the majority of my using alone and hated myself more and more. I was a shell of the person I once was. My eyes were cold, and I lost any interest in showing love or affection.

Change is exciting when you choose it, but horrible when it's chosen for you. In the early morning of July 2, 2001, before the sun came up, there was a knock on my bedroom door. In a doped haze, I opened the door to find two enormous men hovering over me. My mom and dad were standing behind the two giants and an eerie sense of fear and sadness filled me. Intuitively I knew my parents had hired these men to take me to rehab. My parents had tears streaming down their faces as they hugged, trying to offer each other some sort of solace from their despair. I felt only anger and self-pity. The last thing I said to my parents as the giants took me to their truck was, "Fuck you. You've just lost your son."

In the truck, I wouldn't allow myself to ask where we were going for fear that they might think I cared. They handcuffed me to the middle seat after I tried jumping out the window. They put a yellow sign around my neck with big red lettering "Minor in Transit" and walked me through the airport. I yelled and screamed, saying "They're kidnapping me, help, help." People looked with curiosity and apparently didn't feel the need to come see what was going on once they saw the yellow sign. The escorts later told my parents they had never transported a more destructive teen.

Two hours later, I landed in Utah. The man who met me at the airport told me I was going to a wilderness/boot camp/rehab. The horror of my reality started to hit me and I exploded into a full-blown panic attack. This was the one time in my life I sincerely considered suicide. The idea of a life without drugs or alcohol was unimaginable. I couldn't fathom a life without them, and I didn't want to.

The physical withdrawal from drugs is an extremely painful and uncomfortable process. Trying to withdraw while hiking all day and sleeping on the ground is an experience I never want to experience again. I entered the wilderness weighing a frightening 99 pounds. Hiking about ten miles per day with an 80-pound backpack made the process seem unbearable. Many times, it was the recollection of how miserable I was that kept me from a relapse. The phrase *This is an accident, I was never supposed to end up here* played in my mind on repeat. This time the reality was all too clear—I didn't have anyone or anything to put the blame on, other than me and my actions.

The quiet of the wilderness was deafening. The lack of stimuli and distractions was difficult to cope with. Without them, I had to deal with me. Seeing clearly that I was an addict and my life was completely run by chasing a high was undeniable. The only hope for my life to take a turn for the better was to get off the drugs and stay sober. And in my acknowledgment of this indisputable reality, the awful quiet became viscerally calming for me. The old pine trees taught me patience and the abundant sage taught me about effort and consistency.

I started meditating every morning and evening. I would sit between five and ten minutes and get up when I was sufficiently distracted or bored. I also held a belief in God and prayed multiple times a day asking for his or her help in keeping me sober once I got out of treatment. Since then my theological beliefs and understanding of religion have changed dramatically, but I must acknowledge that prayer was immensely helpful. It served as a tool to view my mind, actions, and situation from a different perspective, one that was more objective and one that offered just enough space where I could begin to learn how to self-correct.

The three months I spent in the wilderness gave my brain the opportunity to see the world without the fog of drugs for the first time. I had come to the conclusion that I simply could not touch drugs. I believed that my recovery was going to be contingent upon my spiritual practice and connection. I still had not been introduced to the disease concept of addiction nor the 12 steps and still felt and thought I was broken and no one would ever be able to relate to my struggle with addiction. But I had hope, for the first time in my life.

Once I got home and started outpatient rehab, I was introduced to the 12 steps and was taught about "the phenomenon of craving."

The idea that I could be aware of my thoughts and feelings, recognize the certain combination of them as craving, and not confuse them with reality was life changing.

For the first time, I began to observe the mind and was able to choose to believe it or not.

I dove into the 12-step program. I attended a meeting every day, had a sponsor, worked the steps, and did my best to be of service. I felt very comfortable within the fellowship of 12 steppers. They had an understanding of the hell we had all gone through and a shared appreciation of the freedom from addiction.

Similarly, the inventory process—sharing my fears and secrets—freed my heart and I felt released from the death grip of shame and self-hatred. The amends process, admitting when I made mistakes and committed to righting those wrongs, humbled me. Every morning, I felt that I was a full participant in my life and was shaping the person I wanted to be. I spent the first few years of my recovery in the 12-step world.

Throughout this time, I had been practicing meditation and was deeply committed to a spiritual tradition of an Indian guru. After many years of devoted practice, I developed a crisis of faith. I could no longer subscribe to the theological ideas that I had been practicing. As I looked into my actions and my beliefs, I only found holes. I denied that grace was bestowed upon me, that some superior being had the ability to "grant me serenity or courage." I began to see I had a fundamental disagreement with that idea. I constantly heard people say that their sobriety was a "gift," which I viewed increasingly as a cop-out. My spiritual path and practice needed an update. These beliefs and practices served me very well in the beginning of my sobriety, but now it felt like they were holding me back. In shedding the idea of a god or influential higher power, I was able to take full responsibility for all the happiness and the suffering in my life. I will forever be grateful to the

12 steps for helping me achieve and maintain sobriety. I'll also feel an undying gratitude for the steps as they created the foundation for me to find the Dharma.

Sobriety helped me stop creating wreckage; the Dharma gave me tools to achieve levels of contentment and happiness I thought not possible. I rediscovered something I had learned before I got sober, the Four Noble Truths. While so many other religions or spiritual teachings seemed to tell me that everything was "just the way it's supposed to be," "everything is love," or "God works in mysterious ways," the Four Noble Truths recognized life's unsatisfactory nature and openly admitted that there was indeed suffering. This spoke to the depth of my experience. It was refreshingly honest. I remember thinking, *Finally, a spiritual path that doesn't lie to me.*

Everything in the Four Noble Truths seemed to have been written specifically for me. It was as if I had known these things all along, I just needed to be reminded of them. There is suffering in this always-changing, temporary universe in which we live. The root cause of suffering is greed, hatred, and delusion. I was hooked!

I read every Dharma book I could get my hands on. The theoretical framework of how to view the world was as freeing as it was counterintuitive. It was a crazy idea to not hate pain and not grasp for more pleasure. Trying to meet pain with compassion and pleasure and appreciation and knowing that this too shall pass were tall orders.

I began practicing mindfulness. Just like watching a craving come and go, I applied the tool of observation and investigation to everything. I learned that my heart could be trained. That if I practiced kindness toward myself and others, my experience of life would be happy.

I was not asked to take anything on faith. In fact, I was encouraged to put everything under scrutiny. Everything that the

Dharma told me was true, and I could verify through my own, direct experience if I looked carefully. Through my investigations, I found a new appreciation to leading an ethical life. With increased mindfulness, I was able to see the power of my actions. When I took unethical actions, I created inner turmoil as a direct result. When I took ethical ones, I felt a new freedom that is often referred to as the feeling of blamelessness.

As I continued to immerse myself in the Dharma, I saw that my motivation for continuing my sobriety had changed. Initially, my decision to stay sober was driven by the fear of falling back into addiction and its inevitable hell. After reading about Dharma, the Four Noble Truths, my decision was no longer fear based. It was made every day to affirm life. I injected the dope fiend work ethic of always looking for what I can get into my meditation practice. I learned that no matter what, everything (and everyone) could teach me. Just like a thief was always looking for what he could steal, I began to look for what lessons I could take. The more I practiced embodying compassion and actually believing myself to be worthy of forgiveness and worthy of happiness, the more I saw that there was no need to defend or protect my heart. Being the person I was felt safer and safer.

The Buddha's equation to end suffering has proved itself to be absolutely true and trustworthy. I have every confidence that the Dharma can be applied to addiction.

Today, my mind continues its playdate with madness. And by no means am I a saint. The mind's not the problem, however; it's how I relate to it. Nothing about me is broken. I just need to locate and listen to what is asking for healing. My happiness is not dependent on the situations I find myself in, but the quality of my presence. Remembering that love is always the logically correct response to anything, I let go. Over and over again. My practice is simply to remember that more quickly.

17

Dave

I was introduced to the Dharma and the practice of mindfulness meditation long before I became a full-blown addict and alcoholic. It was the fall of 1993, my first year out of high school. I had my own apartment and was playing in a ska-punk band, drinking in the bars, and having a wonderful time. I smoked good weed every day and enjoyed the occasional hit of acid. I didn't have a care in the world. After being totally confused, angry, and lost throughout my teens, I was starting to feel like things were finally going my way. For the first time in my life, I had some hope for what the future might hold.

I fell madly in love with a girl, my roommate. Things were going great. About three weeks into the relationship, however, we were run down by a drunk driver while walking through cornfields at the edge of town. I was thrown over the roof of the car, but my girlfriend wasn't as fortunate. She was killed on impact. I was devastated beyond belief. I couldn't even begin to fathom "why" this had happened. I immediately lost all sense of hope or meaning in life.

This type of loss had become a theme in my life. My sister was killed in a car accident when I was eleven. Four years later, my favorite uncle died tragically in a bike accident. And now this. I was done. I was so confused and so angry. Worst of all, I was taking it all very personally, a habit that was becoming deeply rooted in my psyche.

I continued to play the scene over and over in my head. I couldn't sleep. I had a hard time focusing at work, and I was experiencing a growing hatred toward life and the world at large. It was bad.

I was lucky enough to have a friend whose mom had a lot of compassion and understanding for my suffering. She encouraged me to meet with one of her close friends, a Dharma teacher. His name was Steven Smith. We met in the morning and talked for a few hours about my life, my experiences and my suffering. He spoke in great detail about the First Noble Truth, the truth of suffering and how meditation can be used to help ease suffering. He invited me to meet him later that day for meditation instructions.

A few hours later, I found myself sitting across from him in the Dharma hall at the Insight Meditation Society (IMS). He showed me how to sit and offered me the initial instructions to bring my attention to the sensation of "the in-and-out breath." I reluctantly gave it a try. I continued to practice mindfulness of breathing for the next few minutes, and I started to feel more at ease. I began to find moments where everything appeared to be okay. Then Steven instructed me, "When you notice your mind begin to wander, gently return to your breath, back to the present moment." This basic instruction blew me wide open. I could actually see that my attention was getting pulled into so many different directions: the stories of my life, reliving the accident, all the horrible experiences, all the anger, the confusion, the pain and sadness. It was all inside my own mind.

As I continued to readjust my attention out of my thinking mind and into my sitting, breathing body, I started to find some relief, at least for one moment. My breath was totally reliable, safe, and available. I spent most of that day sitting and walking, following the same basic instruction. Of course my mind would wander off back into the suffering mind—all the past pains, the stories, the memories, the self-judgment, and the forecasting into the fears and uncertainty of the future—but I could really see, for the first time, that there was a way out.

I felt a tremendous weight come off me that day. I continued to experiment with mindfulness, and it continued to work.

The big message I took away from that initial experience was that there is suffering in life, but that's okay. It's not my fault, and I don't have to continue to suffer if I don't choose to. I could also see mindfulness letting me decide what I paid attention to. I started to become much more aware of my mind's tendency for anger and self-judgment. I eventually learned that I could ignore my mind, and, most of all, I came to understand that I wasn't my mind. That was a major fucking relief; one noble truth down, three more to go.

Six months after Steven introduced me to the Dharma, I participated in my first ten-day meditation retreat. Practicing mindfulness and learning about the Dharma provided me with some ease with the day-to-day struggles of my life. At the same time, I also continued to enjoy drinking, doing drugs, having sex, playing rock and roll, and doing whatever the fuck I felt like doing. I had gotten an insurance settlement from the accident, so I didn't need to work. I mostly just hung around town and in my apartment listening to records, reading Dharma books and books about beat writers and existential philosophy. And for the most part, I was having a great time.

As I continued to sit retreats in the summers and as I grew more familiar with the basic ideas of the Buddha's Dharma, I started to lose the thread. Quite a lot of it didn't make any sense to me. Especially the Second Noble Truth. How could craving cause suffering? I definitely didn't see how that was true. If I had a craving, I would just satisfy it. It was that simple. Maybe reading Dharma books and Bukowski novels at the same time wasn't the best move, but I also had other suspicions about the Dharma. I couldn't really get behind the idea of this loving-kindness toward all beings. I really felt like it was every man for himself. If you are suffering, that's your problem, not mine.

Of course the idea of the fifth precept was completely off the table. To abstain from substances that cloud the mind? Sorry, Buddha, you got your path, and I got mine. I live in America, where satisfying your desire is right at your fingertips. Craving wasn't a problem; *not* satisfying the craving was the problem. As time went on, I continued to question the teachings and felt like they were just some ancient mumbo jumbo that had no real practical application in modern American culture.

I rarely did any sitting practice and would only go on retreat if there was some calamity or chaos going on in my life. My band was becoming more and more successful, and I was growing more and more dependent on drugs, alcohol, praise, and attention. I was really cocky and thought extremely highly of myself; greed and delusion were taking some deep roots in my psyche, and it felt just fine to me. I was starting to feel invincible.

In 1997, with the growing success of ska-punk bands like Rancid, Big Fish, and the Dance Hall Crashers, my band thought we could do well on the West Coast, so we moved out to San Francisco. We were such fools; we had no idea what we were getting ourselves into. It was the peak of the dot-com craze, and everyone and their brother was moving out to the Bay Area. It was impossible to get an apartment, and, if you got one, you couldn't afford it anyways. It was nuts.

Worst of all, nobody in San Francisco gave a rat's ass about our music. Everyone was into metal, hardcore, and street punk.

We were not met with open arms.

About two months into our stay there, our drummer decided to call it quits and move back east. I was growing resentful toward the other members of the band, so I took it as an opportunity to quit too. It was over that quickly.

I was relieved to move on without the dead weight. Besides, I still had the money from my settlement and a good knack for selling weed. I knew I'd be just fine. *Fuck those guys,* I thought. *Every man for himself. If this town wants to hear metal, punk, and hardcore, well, then that's what I'll do.*

I immediately began writing songs and hooked up with a few guys from back east who had also moved out west. We started a three-piece hardcore band called Downright. The drummer of the band also let me move into his van, which didn't run, but was parked down in the Mission District. All I had to do was roll it across the street every few days so he wouldn't get a ticket. I was happy to move into my new home and fulfill my dream of becoming a full-fledged street punk.

During this time, I decided to go ahead and throw cocaine and meth into the mix, which really upped the ante. It was also becoming a bit of a drag sleeping in the van. A good meth bender let me stay up for several days on end. Besides, everyone else was doing it, so I didn't see why it was such a big deal. Meth also allowed me to drink and drink and get into all kinds of adventures roaming the streets of San Francisco, looking for all-night shenanigans.

Sometimes, if we got bored, my friends and I would roll down to the Tenderloin, another San Francisco neighborhood, and drink "cold tea" and eat donuts with the Filipino-tranny-prostitutes just off their nightly shifts. I liked listening to their stories about how they'd show their penises to businessmen after they had paid them $250 for oral or anal sex, laughing as the traumatized businessman figured out he'd just had sex with a man! Those stories never got old, especially after being up for seventy-two hours. It was surreal

and exciting; I was starting to like how "freaked out" I could get.
It was a starting to become a drug in and of itself.

Good times and freak shows aside, this kind of lifestyle was getting old, fast. It barely lasted two years. I started to get a little bit
too "freaked out" with the late-night meth crowd and unsuccessful attempts to get a band off the ground. Not to mention living
on random couches and crashing in the van. Walking the streets
at sunrise and seeing the tweekers roaming about, it was like a
George Romero movie at times. It was fucking gross.

Fortunately I could see the expiration date of it all; I knew it
wasn't for me. I was twenty-two years old and I had no idea what
the fuck I was doing. It was suffering all over again; however, this
time it was my fault, my own doing. I was so confused and disappointed. I had no idea what to do, so I moved back home, back in
with Mom and Dad.

For the next two years, I was totally depressed. I was living back
in Northampton, Massachusetts, working construction, getting
drunk every day and every night. I was miserable and really lonely.
It was the only time in my life where I can honestly say I contemplated suicide.

During this dark time, I slowly started to reconnect with my
old bandmate, Geoff, who was still living out in San Francisco. We
spoke on the phone and, eventually, reconciled. Geoff wanted to
move back to Boston and start the band back up. He wanted me
to join him. I was pretty stoked on the idea of doing something
different and getting the fuck on out of where I was. I decided to
go for it. I moved to Boston in 1999 to give music another chance.

Going to Boston proved to be the best idea. The band got great
gigs right off the bat. Because of the success of the Bosstones, we
were a perfect fit in the Boston music scene. We quickly became a
local success, practically overnight. We landed a record deal with a
new label, which had offices in Amsterdam and Los Angeles. What

a relief; I was back to my old business of selling weed, hanging in the bars, and running my mouth. I was back on top, and I felt truly alive again.

I even went back to IMS to sit a ten-day retreat and began doing some sitting practice every day. There was a meditation center in Cambridge called CIMS and I would drop into a weekly class every now and then. I was having a lot of fun in Boston; things were going my way. It was one big party, and I loved every minute of it. We recorded our first album, hooked up with a booking agent, and jetted off to Amsterdam for our first big European tour. I couldn't have been happier.

When I got to Amsterdam, I was a kid in a candy store. The band was dead serious about partying. Alcohol, weed, and hash became as regular as breathing. I can now honestly say I was a full-blown alcoholic. I had to drink first thing in the morning. If I was awake, I had a drink in my hand. While we were playing gigs we always had at least two or three cases of beer per night and sometimes a bottle or two of wine, vodka, and other booze. People in the venues would also go out of their way to get me pot, hash, and, on occasion, good pills. Once in a while I would even get some blow.

When you are on tour, there's a ton of downtime. You spend a lot of time sitting in a van, a hotel lobby, or a room in the back of a venue. It's really not as great as one would think. The highlight of the day was always the hour on stage playing through our set. I still had a deep love for music, and we played in front of some big crowds right off the bat. I did my best to squeeze every good moment out of the show, because when it was over, it was back to twenty-three more hours of the same old, same old. Things are never as great as you think they will be, you know? My whole life I longed so deeply to play the big shows, in front of the big crowds. I had such wonderful ideas and delusions about how awesome that would be. How great I would feel. I can still remember how lonely I felt the first time I played an open-air outdoor show in front of twenty thousand people. What a fucking letdown that was.

For the next two and a half years or so, I traveled back and forth between Amsterdam and Boston with the band. It was a time of great celebration and partying, accompanied by intense feelings of loneliness and regret—confusion at its finest. I slowly started to isolate myself from my bandmates. I often booked my own hotel room.

I also started taking advantage of Amsterdam's Red Light District. The alcohol and drugs just weren't cutting it on most days. At first I was just going to live sex shows and strip clubs, but it wasn't very long before I started having sex with prostitutes. Once I started crossing those kinds of lines, every fragment of my humanity started breaking down. It was both exhilarating and horrifying; it was addictive.

At one point I decided to stay in Amsterdam while the rest of the band headed back to Boston for a much-needed break in between tours. That's when I began to experience the full implications of the Second Noble Truth—that craving causes suffering.

My life had become a desperately inescapable process of craving-delusion-grasping-suffering, over and over again. My addiction never satisfied me, but it always carried the promise of satisfaction. It was all coming to an end, and I knew it. I tried to suppress it from my awareness, but I just couldn't. I hated everyone in my band. I rarely enjoyed playing shows. I hated myself, and I hated being alive. I remember walking back to my hotel after a long night of drinking, doing shitty drugs, taking sex stimulants, and still not being able to get an erection. I had to walk out on a prostitute.

I went and sat on a park bench and lost my shit. I started bawling my eyes out. How did I let it get this bad? Didn't I know any better? What the fuck? I can't do this shit anymore; I am done. It was like the four horsemen rode in that night to save me: terror, frustration, bewilderment, and despair. Two noble truths down, two to go.

I woke up the next morning and I couldn't shake off this feeling. Nor did I want to. I needed this rare opportunity to muster some sense of meaning or hope or whatever. I purchased two bottles of Guinness, which I drank in the park, thinking. It was my only form of meditation at that point. The truth was obvious but real hard to accept. I needed to get out. I needed to quit the band. *Fuck all of this,* I thought. *I'll go back to Massachusetts and work it out. I'll go on staff at IMS and sit the three-month course. Then I'll go to Burma and become a monk.* Well, maybe not that.

My mind become flooded with thoughts and options, some bad, some good, some realistic, some not so much; it didn't really matter because I knew I would be okay. I'd been through a lot of shit already. I was a tough kid, and I was better than all of this. I was going to be just fine. For sure, I thought. I just needed to figure out my next step. The next few weeks weren't easy but I had made it out alive, mostly because I got drunk and stayed drunk. That was the only way I knew at the time to manage the fear, anger, guilt, and shame. Any good drunk knows that. But I eventually made my way back to Boston. Quitting a successful band with strong label support, a new record, a booking agent, and the potential for a sustained career was one of the hardest things I ever had to do. But I knew it was necessary. Doubt and fear filled my mind, but they had no ground, no aggregate from which to cling. I didn't know much, and I had no idea what I was going to do next, but I knew deep down that I could no longer continue living this way. Long story short, I just did it. I called Geoff, my closest friend for a decade, my bandmate and my biggest resentment. I hated him so much. I showed up at his place with a six-pack of Budweiser. My heart was pounding in my chest; I was scared to death. Halfway through my first beer I just looked at him and said. "I am quitting the band. It's over. I am not having any fun. I hate all of it, and that's that."

Geoff made a few bold attempts to change my mind, but he could tell I was serious. He just looked at me and said, "Get the fuck out of here." I was so happy and relieved to hear him say that. I walked outside and threw up in the bushes; my head was spinning, and my heart was filled with appreciation. It was over that quick!

Later that night, I went out to celebrate with some friends. I just wanted to get loaded and marinate in the joy and sense of newfound freedom. After the bars closed, I went over to a friend's house. I was definitely drunk, but I felt very confident, very clear-headed, very sure of myself in a way that I hadn't experienced in years. It was a strange few minutes. I walked over to the fridge and took out a beer, opened it, and took a few pulls. I started looking around the apartment. It was a mess: empty bottles everywhere and that gnarly aroma of bong water. I knew I didn't want to be there. I took one more sip of my beer and said to myself, *Fuck this too; it's time to move on.*

If I could quit the band, I could quit anything. I put the can of beer down on the coffee table and walked out of the apartment. I have never had a drop of alcohol since that day. That was almost ten years ago.

The next day I caught a ride out to western Massachusetts and went to my parents' house. I told them I had quit the band and that I wanted to get sober. I could see the look of relief on my mom's face. It was a heavy moment. There I was, back at Mom and Dad's, twenty-eight years old. I had no money, a few guitars, and a dirty bag of laundry. I couldn't have been happier.

I started going to 12-step meetings immediately. I struggled and squirmed with all of it. The steps, sponsorship, God, service commitments? I wasn't looking for any of that. I was going to hold off on all of that for just a bit. I wasn't convinced about any of it. Besides, I was a Buddhist and was certainly way above all of this crap. Or so I thought.

I decided it was time for me to get enlightened. I signed up for the three-month course at IMS. I figured that would just about do the trick. In the fall of 2003, with ninety days of sobriety under my belt, I entered into the innermost nether regions of my heart and mind, where I spent the next ninety days. There is really no need to get into the details, and I honestly can't recall anything that profound to report, but I can say I experienced moments of great joy and deep concentration, and times of total despair, anger, fear, and confusion. I got it all, except I was definitely not enlightened. I was mostly filled with a deep and lonely sense of doubt and unworthiness. I was mostly just overwhelmed and completely confused as to what I was going to do next.

On the last day of the retreat, as we were packing up and getting ready to leave, a woman from the retreat told me about Noah Levine. She spent about three minutes giving me his entire biography and recommended I look him up. She also told me Noah had just written a book called *Dharma Punx*. I mostly just blew it off but thought it was interesting that there was a punk rock Dharma teacher out there.

On my ride home I stopped in Amherst to get a real cup of coffee and maybe buy a book. I walked up to Food for Thought bookstore and there it was, right in the fucking window, *Dharma Punx*! Stuff like that never happens to me. I was pretty stoked. Obviously, I bought a copy and raced home to read it. Keep in mind, I hadn't read anything in three months, so I was pretty primed. I got back to my parents' house and read the whole book, front to back, devouring it! It was unbelievable. Finally, someone in the realm of

Dharma who spoke my language and had been through so much of the same shit. I was relieved, inspired, and even a bit overwhelmed. I slept like a rock that night. I do remember that.

The next morning I found the Dharma Punx website and sent Noah an e-mail, a very long e-mail. I included my phone number and told him I would love to talk to him. On some level I hoped he would ask me to come to New York City and join the revolution or some shit.

But that is not how it went. Noah and I talked about recovery and how hard it was to sort out all your shit. I remember complaining about the 12 steps and how much of it seemed like bullshit. Noah told me that he had gotten a lot out of working them over the years and suggested that I be open-minded about it. I think he said something like, "You should go to those meetings, get a sponsor, and work all 12 steps. It will be a good spiritual practice for you." I was pretty disappointed. I think I even went back through *Dharma Punx* and reread the parts where Noah mentioned getting clean. There was no denying the fact that he had put a lot of time into his recovery. Noah had been clean for more than a decade. I only had six months.

Noah also went out of his way to point out that even though I had just sat for three months, I was still pretty crazy. I was still suffering quite a lot. He was real straight up about it, no candy coating. He wished me luck and told me to feel free to stay in touch. For some reason I really responded to everything he had to say. I trusted his experience.

I spent the remainder of that winter traveling around some. I went down to the Caribbean with my friend's family and moved one of their cousins across the country. It was a good time, and I was often in deep reflection about my next move. I decided I would stay with my parents and do the 12-step thing. I figured it was time, and I had to admit it was starting to help me. I was still kind of pissed at Noah for telling me the truth, which has since become an ongoing ritual.

I spent the next five years committed to the 12 steps and embracing a life of recovery and sobriety. It was a great thing; I learned a lot about myself through the 12 steps, and most of all, I learned the power of taking action. I became responsible for my actions. I let go of my resentments and became willing to do the right thing, even when it was the hard thing. Another thing that helped me was recognizing a lot of similarities between the 12 steps and the Dharma. They seemed to be pointing to the same thing, that to be free in this world we would have to overcome the habitual tendencies of greed, hatred, and delusion. We would have to cultivate a way of living that moved us in that direction. I was beginning to find a lot of benefit and freedom with this new way of life.

I started a residential concrete business, got married, and built a house. I was truly embracing my blue-collar roots. I got up every day and went to work, paid taxes, and was a contributing member of society—something I had always avoided. I spent a lot of time with my mom and dad, who lived right down the street. I was real happy for the most part. During that time, I rarely did any meditation practice and attended no retreats. I was finding much more relief working my recovery program. I started to think that Dharma practice was for the overeducated college type, not for a simple drunk like me. I became very proud of my newfound work ethic and blue-collar mentality. But underneath it all, something was missing and I knew it. I had started writing a lot of songs; I was really getting into Johnny Cash and other old-school country artists. I was falling in love with salt-of-the-earth songs about pain, redemption, and forgiveness; songs about overcoming the hardships and struggles of life. I began learning how to play country rhythms on the guitar and learning how to play upright bass. I was on fire for music all over again. I really wanted to give it another shot.

In 2008, my wife and I decided to pack it up and move down to Nashville. I had a few friends down there and I had visited a few times and really fell in love with the city. I was looking forward to getting away from the Northeast's winters and my long work hours pouring concrete. I had high hopes for a better quality of life in the South. I was eager to start a new chapter.

I was in Nashville for less than two months when everything completely went to hell. My whole world began to crumble. My wife, who I had gotten sober with, started drinking again. She told me she wasn't happy with our marriage and that she didn't love me anymore. She had been going out at nights and getting pretty good and drunk. She admitted to sleeping with other people. I was totally out of my mind. We had just moved and now all of this? You got to be kidding me? What the fuck? I took the good advice of my old sponsor, got an attorney, and filed for divorce. I had been living in Nashville for about ten weeks at this point. I didn't even know what to think, or do. I was devastated.

There I was, five years sober, dealing with a painful divorce. I was broke, angry, and scared, and I felt really alone and abandoned. I tried not to blame myself, but it was hard. I had left my house and my successful business back in Massachusetts. Now I didn't have shit.

My reality was like a bad country song and yet I somehow maintained a positive attitude through most of it. I started to plug into the recovery community in Nashville and went to a ton of meetings. I was connecting to new people. To get my mind settled, I returned to daily sitting practice with a vengeance. It was a struggle at first, but fortunately I began to find some ease within the practice. I started to have some hope. Having a hard time making ends meet, I soon found myself working with teenagers at a residential drug and alcohol treatment center, a job I took out of sheer desperation. Part of my job working with the youth was leading recovery groups, which was very challenging at times. On Sunday mornings I would lead a ninety-minute spirituality group. At first it was excruciating. The kids hated it, which only made me hate it. It was rough.

One morning, I was feeling pretty desperate, so I decided talk about the Four Noble Truths. To my surprise, the group of ten boys really liked it. They were totally engaged, and I was blown away.

For the next several Sundays I would do a group on some piece of Dharma, and the teens and I discussed it. I also started adding mindfulness meditation into the format, and they ate it up. It was really fun and inspiring. I started to design other groups that had some component of Dharma or mindfulness built into it. I was really enjoying the work and seemed to have a good knack for working with these kids. Not to mention it was helping me deal with everything I had been through, I was truly being of service.

During that time, I had also reconnected with Noah. He and I finally got to meet in Los Angeles when I attended the Buddhist Recovery Conference at Against the Stream. I was very excited about the emergence of Dharma with Refuge Recovery. The entire conference was empowering, and I felt like I had found a new career path, one that I had never even considered or even thought was possible.

I decided to sign up for Noah's yearlong facilitator training, which lead me to start a weekly sitting group in Nashville. It was a real slow go at first, but over the course of the year, people really started showing up. I had a fairly strong group of about ten to fifteen people and I enjoyed teaching meditation and heart practices. I also felt engaged with learning about the Dharma. I put a lot of time into my talks, read a lot, and listened to Dharma seed nonstop. It was a really wonderful and inspiring time for me. I had a lot of gratitude toward the practice, Noah, and the ongoing potential to witness a growing and thriving Dharma community in Nashville. It was all unfolding very organically.

I graduated from the facilitator program in January 2011. I decided to attend a bunch of retreats that year to deepen my practice. I sat for ten days with Ajahn Succito at IMS. I attended a Secular Buddhist retreat with the Batchelors. I volunteered at the IMS teen retreat and sat for five days with Against the Stream in Joshua Tree. It was one of the best and transformative years of my life.

I also felt locked in and unsupported with my work at the treatment center, so I quit. I started operating programs under the Mind Body Awareness Project (MBA). I began teaching mindfulness to a wide variety of at-risk populations. I started going into the local jails, youth detention, rehabs, and any place that would let me in the door.

In 2012, I taught more than 250 mindfulness classes, provided trainings, and continued to lead weekly Dharma groups. I also started Refuge Recovery meetings at our center, where we now have three per week. Dharma and recovery have become my livelihood and I couldn't be happier. I remember years ago Joseph Goldstein told a story about Munindra, his first teacher. Joseph said that Munindra would often say, "The Dharma takes care of those who take care of the Dharma," words that have always lived somewhere inside my heart. I can tell you with all honesty and humility that those are words I have come to live by. Not because I want to, but because I have to. It's really that simple.

18

Mary

I grew up in New York City with a schizophrenic mother. It had an impact. My dad passed away when I was five, and my two older brothers had already moved out of the house. So it was just me, my mom, and a scary and overwhelming world.

Everything was my responsibility, but I didn't know what to do. For a while Mom was somewhat functional, at least on the outside, but the house was always falling apart, a disaster that I couldn't handle. I couldn't allow anyone to know that my mother was the way she was and that our house was horrific. I kept the outside world and world inside my house separate and made sure the two would never meet. The more the house's walls started to fall down around me, the quicker I built my figurative inner walls at a very early age to protect myself. The inside world of my emotions moved behind this wall because no one could ever, ever know anything about that either. Ever.

I see pictures of myself at age seven. They show a little girl getting plumper and plumper. They show a little girl who found refuge in food.

I remember going to the corner market and buying candy bar after candy bar. The man behind the counter looked at me and said he hoped the candy was not all for me. I lied and said, "No." I had found solace in food, and hiding and shame followed me there.

By the time I was a teenager, my mother's paranoid schizophrenia had taken its final hold. She lived on the couch and listened to the messages on the TV. She believed people were keeping her riches from her and that the comedians on TV were making jokes at her expense. When I broke my arm, she thought I did it on purpose, so the hospital could get some money from her. She was my responsibility and my fault. It was such a mess I barely survived high school. I honestly don't know how I did.

After graduation, my brother invited me to come live with him and his new wife in San Jose. I said yes, and they sent me a plane ticket. I left New York, left my mom by herself, and went to the Promised Land. Northern California in the early 1970s was party central. I was eighteen, my brother and his friends were thirty, and I immediately became grown up. Everything was wonderful. I no longer stuffed my face to fix the pain. But there were bottles of wine, tequila and whites, sheets of acid and kilos of dope. I thought I was in heaven.

In California, I started to get my life together. I got a job and went to college. But my drinking and drug use really took off there. I was in a relationship with a guy who liked to drink as much as I, so everything seemed fine for a while. But the walls I had put in place when I was a kid were pretty solid by then. I had no idea how to be in a relationship. I kept waiting for him to read my mind. Needless to say, it didn't work out.

I went off to Israel with a group of people from the California State University system and proceeded to party for a year. But when I got back, I stumbled along into a dysfunctional relationship for a couple of years. I would take the car and drive up to the redwoods and dream of being anywhere but where I was. I drove and I drove, but it was never far enough away. I was drinking, but food had come back as a way to cope. After two years, the relationship ended, and I graduated from college at that time. I hadn't figured out what else to do, so I kept on going to school.

I moved to Los Angeles, where I studied archaeology at UCLA. Somehow I earned my master's degree, so I kept trudging on in the Ph.D. program. But drinking a whole bunch every day and graduate academics didn't mix well, and drinking won out more and more. I knew I was an alcoholic, but I told myself it was okay because I was not hurting anyone but myself.

Around this time, I got arrested for drunk driving and was sentenced to attend some 12-step meetings. I went because I had to and kind of enjoyed them, but the word *God* made my skin crawl. I knew it worked for others, but I was not interested. I had gone to Catholic school for twelve years, but I turned my back on a god at an early age because it never made sense to me. The idea of a life without drinking was unfathomable, so I kept on, again rationalizing that I wasn't hurting anyone but myself.

I started falling behind in school and, when I was offered a full-time job, I snapped it up. I told my professor I was taking some time off, but for all intents and purposes, I closed the door on archaeology, something I loved. I told myself it was no big deal and drank more to forget about it.

I started living in a little single apartment. I was on my own for the first time. And my life got smaller. I went to work in the morning, came home, drank, and passed out. I would sit and drink and listen to music and tell myself I was happy to be alone, that I didn't need anyone. At work, I perfected a Little Mary Sunshine persona. Everything was always good and wonderful, and I was happy and shiny and perfect. I know in hindsight that I thought I had to be that way to fit in. Any messiness would not be accepted. Any imperfections would be dealt with harshly. Deep inside, I felt very broken, so being alone was my only answer. I could be Little

Mary Sunshine for eight hours a day, and crash and burn for the rest. The walls got taller and thicker.

In spite of my isolation, I got involved with a guy from work. The relationship did not go the way I wanted. We broke up. One night, I found myself setting out to get even with him. I knew how to hurt him and I did. I won't go into all the details, but I do remember realizing the next morning that I had crossed that line. I realized what I had done, how I intentionally hurt him. The lie I had been living, about only hurting myself, had been exposed.

I admitted to him that I was an alcoholic, mostly because I learned that was a good excuse when my behavior was really bad. But something within me had changed, because normally I would disappear from the relationship, and this time I knew I would have to do something about it. I didn't drink for two weeks, which I was proud of. I felt good not being sick and hungover every day. But after two weeks, I grew so uncomfortable in my own skin that even though I didn't consciously feel the desire to drink, I drank anyway. I know today that I took away my only coping mechanism but did not replace it with anything else. The discomfort became too great. I was off and running again.

I needed to get help again so I found myself back in a 12-step program. They still said that word *God,* but this time my skin didn't crawl. I felt some hope. I found myself going back, day after day. And I found that I remained sober.

This recovery program was my lifeline. For my whole life, I had felt the need to keep up a smiley persona on the outside while I hid everything on the inside. The 12-step program showed me I could admit that I needed help without having to open my mouth and actually say the words out loud. That's the best I could do at the time, and it was enough. Slowly, I absorbed what was being said at the meetings and I got involved. I found someone I could trust to work with and I made a commitment to tell her what was going on inside. I heard them say you only had to change one thing, everything, but honesty was what was required.

I found a new way of life and was able to begin the healing journey. As I got more and more involved with meetings and the 12 steps, the fog lifted, which let me see how my fear and my natural instinct for survival created so many of my problems. I started to chip away at the walls that kept me separated from the world. Though I was never able to connect with a Judeo-Christian idea of a god, I was able to define my higher power as a Group of Drunks and I slowly began to trust others. I learned that I was not the center of the universe, and it became a daily task to remember that fact.

From very early on in my recovery, I took some time each morning to be quiet and reflect, sometimes reading or writing or just sitting. At some point, I began a very simple meditation practice of breathing and using mantras such as, "let go." Of course the serenity would disappear once I left my house, but that quiet time has remained a constant in my life.

Life went on, and recovery continued. I got married and held a job. I moved through life with a willingness to change in some respects but was incapable of seeing how to do it. I still thought I had to achieve something to be okay. I had to be the top performer at work. I thought I had to be perfect in my recovery. I thought I had to have the perfect home, and the perfect marriage. I never believed that anything I had, or did, or said, was enough. I always felt like I had to figure out everything in my own head before I made a move. I lived this way without seeing it for many years, experiencing the discomfort of not being enough and still being on the outside looking in.

Along with this sense of inadequacy was a nonstop sound track of comparing and judging. And I was never on the plus side. The walls had diminished a bit, but they were still there.

Even with years of sobriety, I felt trapped at times. I had learned to open up by working with others, but only to a certain extent. It took me a long time to realize how much of an impact my growing up had on me and how thick those walls were and how I hid inside them. I would look around and see others sharing at a deeper level than I could. Women would share things with me I could never dream of telling someone else. I told just enough to get along, and within the prescribed parameters of what a sponsor or sponsee could or should share. Outside of those parameters it was still too scary to open up, too scary to even acknowledge anything.

On the spiritual side of things, I never developed a belief in any kind of god and continued to resist that piece of the 12-step program. I would simply ignore the talk of God, and I still considered my higher power as something over there that I had no clue about but knew it wasn't me. Prayer, so important in 12-step work, was never a tool I used or something that made much sense to me. I had nothing to pray to and did not look to anything divine to fix me.

Sometimes, however, I did feel a momentary sense of calm and ease when I could totally let go into the moment, in spite of what was going on in my life. When I read *Start Where You Are* by Pema Chödrön, I was amazed. I ran around waving the book at everyone and yelling, "This is my program, this is my program."

After nineteen years of sobriety, however, something still wasn't right. I was deep in my program and involved with the group and with others. I worked on so many of my runaway instincts and had built a good life, but there were dark places that had me so very broken. I couldn't explain them. A number of things happened around this time. My outside experiences were good, but inside was bleak and there was still a dramatic separation of the inside and the outside, and I was uncomfortable.

During a regular mammogram, they found a small lump and wanted to do more work. I retreated further inside. I told my husband, but no one else. They did a procedure, but it was inconclusive so they had to do another one, a little more invasive. I still told no one. I didn't even want my husband to come to the hospital. "I'm fine, leave me alone," I told him. I would spend hours in my head dreaming of running away. The thought of dying was actually pleasant. This line of thought made perfect sense.

Leading up to this I had spent almost a year going through Sharon Salzberg's *Lovingkindness*. Every morning, I did the practices, and I noticed a difference in how I felt toward others, specifically people I once felt neutral toward. Wow, this stuff worked. At the end of that year, and around the time of my mammogram, I found the Dharma Punx website and saw an announcement about a New Year's Eve Intention-Setting ceremony. It sounded really good, so I went. The place was packed, and I didn't know a single person there. My intention—to have more compassion for myself—came out spontaneously. I was shocked by the words I heard myself saying but was so touched by my experience that I was determined to go to the weekly meditation classes that Noah Levine had set up in Los Angeles a few months earlier. I went once and knew I could not stop going. My life changed again.

Formal Buddhist practice took the recovery program I had developed through the 12 steps and my own experience and sharpened it to a precision edge. Ideas that were partially formed before, such as staying in the now and being with life as it unfolded, came into focus and were outlined and delineated in such a way that I couldn't imagine this practice not being a part of recovery or of my life. These practices became tools to use to continue the journey. I had been floundering for a few years, and now, finally, the path had been opened. And the work was just beginning.

I have hit wall after wall in practice. Daily meditation and extended periods on retreat have helped melt the barriers that self-preservation built. For the first time, I started to look at the impact my early years had on me, and, through meditation, I was able to sit and begin to see how those experiences conditioned me in a way that I could not have seen otherwise. I had spent my whole life in my head. I kept turning to food or drugs or alcohol to keep the pain away. With meditation I allowed the feelings to arise and learned to be quiet with them. For so many years I had listened to the stories in my head, and although I knew they were false and I tried to power my way through them, I couldn't.

Occasionally I had breakthroughs where the experience moved from the mind to the heart, but here were tools I could use specifically to address my recovery. Not just recovery from my physical addictions, but tools to enable me to heal at a deeper level. The walls I put in place began to dissolve with the patient application of mindfulness. The willingness to look at what arose inside, whether it matched the story in my head or not, was the effort the Buddha talked about that was necessary for liberation.

The Buddha taught that we don't get out of this life without pain, but I had spent my whole life avoiding it. I was diagnosed with the human condition and finally was able to turn and face the pain. The grasping for something out there to fix me was never going to work. Turning inside to heal is where the practice occurs. The first healing was internal. I learned it was not self-indulgent to bring compassion to your own experience. In fact, it was the answer. Not lame, but strong. Oh, who knew? Grief, anger, and shame saw the light of day for the first time, and I welcomed them.

But this is not a practice that promises instant gratification or permanent bliss. As I continue to live and breathe and stay willing, mindfulness and effort allow more insights. I hit another wall a few years later and found that the old ideas of self were still strong. They still kept me from connecting with others. I went into therapy to help me clearly see what was keeping me from other people. Another wall came down.

Nothing in my past has changed. Nothing about my story has changed. What has changed is my ability to see the habitual patterns of thinking that kept me suffering, dissatisfied or stressed, or off-kilter—or however you want to translate *dukkha*. My perception of the facts is ever-shifting. My ideas are dissolving. The practice requires a continual effort to feel whatever arises in each moment. Continued focus on each moment requires more and more subtlety and feeling of each moment. "What is this?" becomes the question of the moment, every moment. And the new response is kindness rather than a search for a way out of the present, however justified it may seem at the moment. It's okay to receive a diagnosis that reads, "Human Condition." In fact, it's the only response that allows the connection with others I didn't even know I was missing.

Today, I continue the work on the path and I continue to uncover my heart's true nature as I cultivate a mind-body connection that responds to life with love and compassion. The judgmental and belittling voices still show up, but I say hello and let them continue on their way. I now feel ease and comfort while experiencing life as it unfolds, along with a deep knowing that drinking or drugging or eating or anything will not fix what's not broken.

19

Pablo

Buddhist practice is, in and of itself, not only totally sufficient to establish and maintain long-term sobriety, but designed precisely to pinpoint and overcome its causes. For me, this isn't just philosophy. It's how I live my life.

I'm an unusual case. My sobriety was established on Buddhist principle and practice alone. As a founding member of the New York City Dharma Punx community, which featured a high concentration of people in recovery, I had the luxury of a community of people in midtransformation who all credited sobriety as part of their spiritual work. But early in my recovery I realized that Alcoholics Anonymous, though an effective system for many people, would not be a match for me. It didn't need to be because the Dharma Punx community and its Buddhist practices would prove sufficient.

My addiction story begins at twelve years old, when I realized I was gay. I was terrified. This was the early 1980s, and I lived in the small military town in the Mojave Desert of California. There was no *Glee* on television. In fact, the only gay person I'd ever seen on TV was a man on the talk show *Donahue* who was dying from AIDS. There was no Internet or "It Gets Better" campaign. Queer issues had not in any way permeated the mainstream. The president, Ronald Reagan, was antigay. My father, a violent man who screamed at the top of his lungs nearly every day, was explicitly homophobic. My friends at school played a game called "smear the queer" during lunch breaks. Being gay in this country, in my town, in my home, made me a target.

The conscious realization that I was gay lasted only a few moments. It was immediately overridden by some protective part of my psychology that said, *There's no way I'm ever telling anybody this*. I literally didn't think about my sexuality until I was nineteen. Nevertheless, it was precisely at that point that the world moved from being a safe place to a profoundly unsafe one for me. I was now vulnerable to being disowned, ostracized, or, worse, the target of violence.

Because I had no authentic self-expression, I had no authentic connection, which left me with deep feelings of isolation. I now know from my three years working at a suicide prevention line for LGBTQ teens that these are the reasons why they want to kill themselves. It's also why queer people have a disproportionate incidence of addiction issues when compared to the general population. Without the agency of authentic self-expression, a lifelong pattern of coping through avoidance, denial, and escape emerges. This turning away from pain is the primary movement of the addictive process, one that Buddhism so boldly corrects.

The dual events of my mother's death from cancer and my younger friend Matthew's death in a bus accident when I was nineteen destabilized me very deeply. Because I was raised an atheist by a father who said that anyone who believed in God was a "fucking idiot," I had no notions of heaven or reincarnation. Death seemed like annihilation. To me, life was being trapped between that void and an unsafe, violent, scary world.

By the time I turned twenty-two, I had already witnessed three murders and one attempted murder on three separate occasions. Two kids were shot in the head at a rave I attended. I had to walk past their bodies to get out. On another occasion, I found a homeless man in an alleyway. He had been staked and set on fire. And once, three men drove up to my neighbor's house looking for a man. When they couldn't find him, they shot his wife through her upstairs window. I remember seeing her several weeks later. Her jaw was caved in, deformed. The images of what I saw continue to haunt me today.

I began to have panic attacks daily, which persisted for more than a decade. Violent images would, and still do, haunt my mind. My siblings were all much older than me, and they were spread out all over the country so I had little contact with them. I felt abandoned, completely on my own to grieve and figure things out. I literally kept my experiences to myself, confiding in no one, partly because I had no model for it, partly because to do so would make the experiences real. At the time, my fragile sanity depended on avoidance. Turning away, not toward.

The traumas prompted a deep internal upheaval in me, which reawakened my conflict about my sexual orientation. Eventually, I came out. My brothers and sisters were largely supportive, but my father disowned me. I spoke to him maybe two more times, in passing, before his death in 2001.

My drinking was more than a "move" away from pain. I jumped ship completely. The pain of "being home" in this body, heart, and mind was so unbearable that I abandoned myself completely and stayed gone for thirteen years. When the cost/benefit analysis of drinking moved too firmly into the "cost" category, I knew I had to stop. When I did, all the pain was there on the other side waiting to finally be tended to. Drinking hadn't worked.

Like most people who decide to get sober, I was brought to Alcoholics Anonymous. While AA certainly works for others, its core propositions felt irreconcilable with my own experiences. I couldn't, for example, rectify the assertion that "alcoholism is a disease" with the facts of my own life.

The idea that by simply attending an AA meeting, without any consultation, one is expected to take on a blanket diagnosis of "diseased addict" was to me, at best, patronizing. At worst, irresponsible. Irresponsible because it doesn't encourage people to turn toward and heal the actual underlying causes of their abuse of substances.

I drank for thirteen years for REALLY good reasons. Among them were unprocessed grief, parental abandonment, isolation, violent trauma, anxiety and panic, social oppression, a general lack of safety, deep existential discord, and tremendous diet and lifestyle imbalance. None of which constitute a disease, and all of which manifest as profound internal, mental, emotional, and physical discomfort, which I sought to escape by taking external substances.

It is only through one's own efforts to turn toward life on its own terms and to develop a wiser relationship to what's there through mindfulness and compassion that make freedom from addictive patterns possible. My sobriety has been sustained by facing life, processing grief, healing family relationships, accepting radically the fact of social oppression, working with my abandonment conditioning, coming into community, renegotiating trauma, making drastic diet and lifestyle changes, forgiving, and practicing mindfulness, to name just a few. Through these things, I began to relieve the very pressure that compulsive behaviors are an attempt to resolve.

This fact calls into question another of the core philosophies of AA: powerlessness. In AA, I heard about how no human power could relieve our alcoholism. Only God could, once we sought him out. But if you experience addiction as I do, as a habitual movement away from pain toward pleasure or numbing, then you see clearly that overcoming addiction depends on cultivating the capacity to be present for pain and to work to reduce its causes. The only person who has the power to do that is you! Your teachers, books, and statues can't do it for you, and God certainly doesn't do it.

I was raised an atheist and came into sobriety without any evidence to sway me from the powerful conditioning of my upbringing. Though I no longer identify as an atheist, believing in God when I was growing up in a country that relentlessly oppresses queer people in the name of God was unrealistic, and the idea of having to now adopt a belief in God to stay sober was insulting. More important, it just didn't seem to have anything to do with establishing and maintaining sobriety. If anything, struggling with the God concept is a distraction from what's actually relevant. A belief in God is absolutely NOT necessary to stay sober.

For me, all of what is necessary to know and practice for successful long-term sobriety is contained within the Four Noble Truths. My friend and teacher, Stephen Batchelor, taught me to think of the Four Noble Truths not as propositions to believe, but rather as tasks to be accomplished. Thinking of the truths as four tasks makes them a practice.

Practicing or "living" the Four Noble Truths can be critically important for someone interested in a Buddhist recovery. The task of the First Noble Truth is to "fully know suffering." Practically speaking, this means we stop running from pain and DO precisely the opposite: we turn toward it and study it and our relationship to it. It means we abandon the delusion that our lives can be all pleasant and no pain. Instead, we acknowledge our lives as a balance of what is beautiful, pleasant, and awe-inspiring and what is unpleasant, painful, and outright traumatizing. That good food, sex, nature, love, and connection are balanced by disease, abandonment, hurricanes, war, and suicide.

In this turning toward, we become grounded, sensitive and

responsive to whatever life brings, instead of ungrounded and reactive. We remain unruffled when difficulties come. In fact, we expect them. One of my clients in my wellness and recovery counseling practice made a brilliant observation. He said, "Addiction is the exact opposite of turning toward suffering." He's exactly right!

And the teaching of the Four Noble Truths is famously referred to as a "middle path," precisely because its "middleness" is defined by two extremes we are advised to avoid, the addictive pursuit of sensual pleasure on one side and self-denial and punishment on the other. Sobriety is a condition that actually makes this "turning toward" possible.

So the task of the First Noble Truth is to expand our awareness to embrace the full range of life experience, including pain. Inevitably, what happens when we expand our awareness is that we start to see our body/mind's built-in tendency to want to get rid of and avoid pain and grasp for and maintain pleasure. These normal internal responses to life are called *craving* in Buddhism, a term used by addicts all over the world but one that is profoundly unexamined.

"The truth of craving" is the Second Noble Truth. Its task is to "let cravings be" as opposed to identifying with and reacting unskillfully to them by drinking and using. When we let them be, they cease, just like everything else in the universe does. They arise, do their dance, and end because they are subject to impermanence.

This ceasing is the Third Noble Truth, the "truth of cessation." It points to both the ceasing of the craving and the ceasing of the pattern of suffering that is the result of identifying with and reacting to craving. The task is to realize its end.

This practice of opening to life on life's terms, of mindfully monitoring the cravings provoked within us as we move through life, while allowing these cravings to arise and pass without the patterned reactivity of addictive behavior, opens up the possibility of a different way of life.

This way of life, the Fourth Noble Truth, is a comprehensive system for conscious living. The Eightfold Path addresses the optimal ways to think about the world and what intentions support freedom from suffering and harm. It addresses our conduct, including our relationship to intoxicants, and offers us the appropriate meditative practices in the service of freedom from the causes of addiction. The Eightfold Path acts as a feedback loop to the other three noble truths in that it deepens one's capacity to practice living them. The message of the Four Noble Truths to the addict is this: **there's no such thing as a life with no pain, and you no longer have to harm yourself in response to it!**

20

Enrique

I've come to understand and believe on one level or another that the story doesn't really matter or at least not the details. Because the external conditions of my story may be different from yours. I like to tell a different story. The story of the heart. Spoken in the language of the heart. Something we may all be able to understand.

I heard this story at my first silent retreat with Against the Stream Buddhism Meditation Society. It's about an amazing clay Buddha statue, which was over ten feet tall and weighed at least two tons. It was kept in a monastery in Thailand, but local developers there were planning to tear down the monastery to make way for a highway. The monks arranged for a crane to come and move the Buddha to its new location. When the crane started to lift the statue, it began to crack. The crew had underestimated its weight. Wanting to protect their statue, the monks must have said something like, "Let's chill out and figure out something else." The crew lowered the statue back down and decided to bring in a more powerful crane the next day. To add insult to injury, the rains came, so the monks had to lovingly cover the statue with tarps to keep the moisture away. They did this loving.

Later that night, the head monk took his flashlight and went out to make sure the Buddha was all right. When the light of the flashlight shone into the crack of the clay, he saw a glimmer . . . a reflection of something underneath that shroud of clay. He started to carefully chisel away shards of clay. The glimmer grew brighter. Hours later, he had chiseled away all the clay to reveal the presence of a Buddha made of solid gold.

The monk went back into the history books and found out that the Burmese army once invaded Thailand. Because their Buddha was made of gold, the monks didn't want the Burmese army to pillage it so they covered the Golden Buddha with twelve inches of clay. Sadly, the monks were slaughtered in the invasion, and the secret of the Golden Buddha stayed hidden for two centuries.

And as new monks and people came through, all they saw was some dusty old Buddha. They didn't realize its value.

So this is my story. This may be your story. Right? No matter where we come from, or the conditions surrounding us, we on some level or another drink and get fucked up on drugs to escape pain, the pain of our past, present, and future. And in doing so we sometimes forget who we are. This story reminds us that we all have intrinsic value. There is nothing wrong with us.

The Buddha started some of his talks with the saying, "Oh nobly born, sons and daughters of the Buddhas of the awakened ones, remember who you really are." He also said that if the element of the truth seeker did not already exist within you, there would be no path, no discovery, no awakening of wisdom, no awaking of compassion. Because the element of truth seeker is within you, there's a part of you that already knows who you are and wants to awaken to this mystery, and because this is a part of you, it takes you on this journey of discovery.

I love that. I believe that. Not only do I believe it, I know it to be true in my very own experience. We've all been hurt, abandoned, let down. We've all felt pain, grief, sorrow. We are so resilient. There is nothing wrong with me. There never was. The fear that something was wrong with me was why I started running away from pain, and why my intentions were so misguided. I was so confused and so afraid of pain that I unskillfully tried to escape it, while what I was actually doing was covering up what was pure and good. And locked inside of me was the very thing I was trying to escape from. What did I want to escape from? The pain of loss and abandonment of my dad not being there. I wanted to escape the pain I felt from the story I made up about how it was my fault he left. That he didn't love me and I was unlovable.

I lived in a dangerous neighborhood, so my mother sent me to live with my grandparents in Arizona at the age of eleven. I felt abandoned and betrayed. I felt unloved and unlovable. And I had a really strong desire not to exist anymore. Around the same time, I took my first hit of weed and drank my first drink. I went from feeling pretty powerless to feeling superpowerful. I felt like I could actually keep going. I didn't care about what had happened to me. I found my medicine. And I felt good, for the first time in a long time. And in hindsight I turned my will and life over to drugs and alcohol. And I wanted to feel good all the time. And the rest of my life was in this effort.

My drug and alcohol use progressed very quickly. And along with this came a criminal lifestyle. By thirteen, I was in a gang. I was constantly getting high and drunk. I soon landed in juvenile hall. In and out and in again, over and over. By sixteen, I was completely gone. The shadow side had taken over. I spent eight months in a locked-down placement home and then became a ward of the state. I get now that all I wanted was to be loved and accepted and had a deep need for community. I was just barking up the wrong tree. Anyway, that's what it looked like. In and out of jail. In and out of homes, letting people down left and right. Hurting the people who loved me the most.

Gnarls Barkley says hurt people hurt people. This was my story. In so much pain that I couldn't hold on to it anymore, I spilled the pain out onto anyone who got close.

Sometimes it's likened to this idea of going to pet a little puppy and the puppy tries to bite you and you get all pissed off. But upon further investigation, you notice the puppy's leg is caught in a trap and is in a lot of pain. And the people who reached out and helped were the very people I attacked.

But I was superrighteous about my drinking and using. I was going to keep drinking no matter what. I found my solution, so why would I let her go? I don't care what you say about me and my mistress, she lets me be me. She never lets me down. She keeps me safe and protected. Until I no longer had a choice.

In the end, it came down to this. I was twenty-four years old and lost. I was supertired, so tired. As they say, I was sick and tired of being sick and tired. I had the delusion that if I could just get what I wanted, if I could just stay high, everything would be okay. But this belief was killing me. I was dying inside. I was losing my mind. I kept wishing that I would just die.

The conditions leading up to my rock bottom looked like this. A year earlier my girlfriend broke up with me. I was at a real bad place then. I was racked with so much pain inside. I looked and felt like shit. Around this same time, I ran into some high school friends I used to party with. They all seemed to be doing really well. They were all graduating from college and getting married. I was humiliated. I lashed out. I beat up my roommate, which got me kicked out of my apartment.

I beat a man unconscious with a mag light. I almost killed him.

I lost $10,000 in a drug deal gone bad, and the people who fronted me the money were after me. I had to go into hiding. I got into a gnarly fight with my dad.

I ended up in jail, which cost me the chance to hang out with my brand-new baby cousin. My only cousin.

This was just a real low point in my life. The fear, shame, guilt, and remorse had taken over. I was scaring the people around me. My mind was in full attack mode. And I went into a deeper hole.

So the very last straw was getting kicked out of a speed den, literally the last place left for me to go. I had to throw my things in a shopping cart and push it down Victory Boulevard, aimlessly walking around the city with thoughts of suicide and homicide. Then, as they say, I had a moment of clear seeing, of clarity.

I landed in a thirty-day inpatient rehab. From there I committed to a year at a sober living home. When I had about eleven months of sobriety and was on my eleventh step, someone handed me *Dharma Punx*. I read it and was immediately hooked. I totally related to the message and became obsessed with meditation.

Now, remember that I was a high school dropout, and the only time I read was in jail when there was absolutely nothing else to do. And I lived in a really small world and knew nothing of eastern philosophy or Buddhism. So I like to think that the Dharma found me.

Eventually I went out and found a home. I found my home. And what really happened was that I continued to show and start to feel. I started to slow down. Meditation has not only brought calm into my heart and mind, but it has allowed me to bring insight into my destructive mental and emotional habits.

In the Big Book of AA it says that drugs and alcohol are merely a symptom of our internal imbalance. The disease centers in our mind.

This is why mindfulness and Dharma are so powerful when it comes to recovery. It gets to the root of what is happening. When I take the time to carefully observe my thought process, I begin to see how I create many of my own problems, and then I can learn to let go.

I think of the three jewels: Buddha, Dharma, Sangha. For me, the metaphor for this path is coming home. Finding refuge in my body, in my heart, loving all of me and trusting in my own potential to be awake, which is what Buddha means. There's a fucking map! It's all laid out for us. I practice and things start getting clearer. I start to see the truth and have tools to help me be a good person.

And there's a community. I'm so grateful I don't have to do this on my own. I know that they've got my back and because of that I can let go, and now, as my friend Pablo says, "Me and my friends are staying free."

21

RuthAnn

I grew up in religion. My parents were part of a large Christian cult/ministry that practiced radical outreach on college campuses all over the United States. I think they really believed they were going to change the world. My dad was fiery and charismatic, handsome and charming. People loved him. People loved my family. I grew up homeschooled and transient, always bouncing from town to town as my dad received preaching gigs.

We eventually landed back in my father's hometown in Tennessee, where we lived with my grandparents. My brothers and I were unceremoniously dumped into public school. This is when I started to have trouble coping. I had been chronically molested by the brother of a playmate before we moved to Tennessee, and insomnia and shame had become part of my life.

I was eight years old and my mind was out of control, especially at night. I remember repeating scenarios over and over and feeling tortured, afraid, and full of self-loathing. I would lie there for hours trying to decide if I should tell my parents what was happening. I started finding ways to avoid my memory. I read a lot. I had story tapes I listened to.

By the time I entered fourth grade, I started feeling different and unacceptable and not as good as others. I cried all the time. I couldn't handle my homework assignments. I felt so inadequate, overwhelmed by fear and longing for things to be different.

Eventually I learned to survive. I made friends. Social acceptance was medicine. I made friends with wealthy girls, girls with horses. I learned to ride and joined 4-H. I always felt like the poor kid the rich folks were helping out. I always felt so scared and longed to fit in, to be good enough.

My father was a youth minister at a "nondenominational" church. It was pretty normal at first, eventually transforming into an evangelical bedlam. Wild sermons about hell and sin, absolution and eternity. I came of age believing my soul was in constant jeopardy, studying my Bible as much as possible and committing to sexual abstinence in hopes of a holy marriage, hoping that would erase how grotesque I felt after what my friend's brother had done to me. These are my first spiritual memories. Longing for God and relief from my guilt and shame. I wanted so badly to feel whole and loved. I truly believed that if I could be good enough, pray hard enough, I would get better. I pretty much always felt bad, though. Depression and anxiety consumed me, as well as my overwhelming longing for love.

As I entered my early teens I began to grow disenfranchised with God and church, along with my father. I started to find more solace and connection in depressing literature and what the church called "secular" music. I had a brief but powerful romance with a boy too old for me, who broke up with me after I failed to sleep with him. I was crushed. It was the beginning of a pattern in my life.

My older brother started drinking heavily by the time he reached high school. I think I was thirteen when he gave me my first drink, and I felt accepted by him and warm inside. Then he got me stoned. I felt special and different. I started drinking and smoking weed whenever I could.

My parents left town one weekend and my brother threw a party. A guy from my church came over, got me drunk, and took advantage of me sexually. The memory of how I shut down emotionally that night is still very clear to me. It was almost a decision to pursue self-destruction. From then on, I was totally committed to my search for nonexistence. Every drug, every man, every thing I could do to get outside myself and not feel. Fuck God. Fuck my parents. Fuck church. Fuck love. Fuck me.

I started working when I was fifteen for a little family-owned restaurant. A lot of the employees were college aged, and I was quickly taken in as part of the group, almost as a pet. House parties and bars were a regular part of life, and, even at that age, I felt totally motivated by my desire to drink. Hanging out with these older people always felt like an opportunity to get fucked up—the beginnings of using people to get what I wanted. Also the beginning of waking up to blurred memories of things I wish I hadn't done. Haphazard blow jobs given to men twice my age or making out with some college guy in front of a video camera. The next day I just pushed all this stuff out of my mind, terrified by it.

Then Isaac entered my life during this time. Isaac was twenty-two, drunk, and a pseudo-rock-star type who lived with his mom. I was drawn to him almost as much as I was to alcohol. We started meeting in secret, fooling around. I would wait and wait to hear from him, and go to meet him and let him touch me and get him off in the back of his stupid van in parking lots, behind gas stations, back country roads. I would go home smelling faintly of sex and the fryer grease from whatever shitty restaurant he was employed at. Sometimes he would show up where we were supposed to meet; sometimes I would just wait and wait, angry and savoring the pain of being wronged when he blew me off.

My parents had no clue I was drinking or in a relationship with Isaac. I had become an expert at hiding and manipulating, giving them what they wanted to hear and see. At home I was getting ready for college. As part of my homeschool education, I was enrolled in community college classes. I was thin and pretty and outgoing and, according to my parents, smart and talented. I worked hard and bought my first car. I was awarded enough scholarship money to pay for nearly all of my university education.

I graduated at seventeen and headed off to a nearby school with zero skills or self-respect and a serious desire to get out of myself. I almost immediately attached myself to the people who provided an environment for getting messed up, which is when I started my drug experimentation. Acid, ecstasy, mushrooms, pills. My second semester I got tangled up with a sweet, gentle, rich, kind cokehead nicknamed Toe, who introduced me to all the wonderful numbing effects of blow. I attached myself to Toe because he provided me with attention and alcohol and drugs. But that didn't stop me from fooling around with other guys. I knew my behavior hurt Toe, but I kept after what I wanted. Party. Party. Party. That's all I wanted.

One night, at a party I left with a friend named Whiskey Ben. I woke up in his bed the next day. Blood covered the sheets. That's how I lost my technical virginity, although my innocence had been gone since I was a child. When I left that early morning, I took the sheets and my nearly empty gallon of Evan Williams. It was a rainy day and I felt nothing.

Despite all my sexual distractions, I stayed in touch with Isaac, always addicted to his unavailability. One night he drunkenly yelled at me over the phone while I was with Toe. I wanted to get back at him. Toe had a jar full of drugs: morphine, Xanax, Adderall, coke, MDMA. He was really absentminded and accidentally threw it away. I remember watching him come out of the Dumpster holding it, victorious. We bought a bunch of booze and really went for it that night. We did all the blow, all the MDMA, then I have vague memories of him chopping up lines mixed with morphine pills and Adderall, and lines of Xanax. At one point I was on my knees in front of the coffee table; he took my hand and asked me to trust him. The next thing I remember was being outside of my body, having a beautiful dream and being alive in it. I don't know how long it lasted. I regained consciousness to Toe crying over me, saying he couldn't get me to wake up, that he picked me up and threw my body around with no result and that he was scared. I came out of my stupor a little and all I could think about was this stupid exam that I had that day, that I had to get to class.

We got into Toe's truck, and he started driving me to campus. He was still pretty fucked up and probably scared about how I had maybe almost died. He looked over at me while he was driving and said, "You are so beautiful." His truck went off the road and he jumped a ditch.

Somehow he still got me to campus, and I ran into my ridiculous Theater Appreciation 101 class, probably answered "C" on all the questions and then ran back out and sat on the ground and cried. I knew something was wrong, that all this behavior was not okay. I briefly tried to just drink, thinking it was all the drugs that were the problem. That lasted maybe a week or two. Things just kept getting worse. I drank harder, kept after the drugs. Fell in with more and more older guys, all of whom would sleep with me until they got tired of me, or my drinking.

I was just eighteen, and guys were already frustrated with my need to bring handles of liquor into the bedroom. This is the behavior I repeated over and over for the next eight years, harming myself with men and sex, covering it up with alcohol. Carving this groove into my heart, making a hard smooth place where nothing could stick or stay—an obsidian surface good for nothing but breaking things.

The end of my spring semester of my freshman year I bought tickets to a concert down in Atlanta. My little brother loved this band, and I got permission to make the four-hour drive. My sixteen-year-old brother and I hopped in my car with these two guys, Joe and Tim. I had just met them. They were strangers, really. I was really nervous, a small-town girl with not much experience driving in big cities. I hated driving even in nearby Nashville. So, obviously, partying on the way down was the best solution for my anxiety. We boozed the whole way. Broke and underage, when we ran out of beer we would just stop at a grocery and steal it. Miraculously, I got us to the venue.

Inside, I bumped into a friend who sold me Adderall. I chopped up a few, snorted them, and convinced him to sell me more than he really wanted to. Feeling more awake, I agreed to go pick up some food with one of the guys and we left my brother with the other dude. Drunk, tired, high on pills, I rear-ended a limo in about eight minutes. Tim's head cracked my windshield. The airbag busted my chin open. Our first thought was the weed we had and all the open beers. We stupidly started tossing beer cans out into the street. I recently found a court document from this incident, and it said, "Defendant Dillon did not inquire about the well-being of the limousine driver, but instead started pouring alcoholic beverages into the street." I got arrested, and Tim went to the show, where he explained what happened to my baby brother. In the back of the cop car I ate all my Adderall. I couldn't believe what was happening to me.

The arrest and subsequent charges just seemed to entangle me more with the crazy lifestyle I was living. It felt like what I deserved. I started to identify more and more with my using lifestyle. Not caring. My best friend at the time, when she would get a little tipsy, liked to say, "This is RuthAnn, she don't give a FUCK, ya'll." "Goddamn RuthAnn" was another nickname I got used to.

My parents let me move home, where I went back to my high school job and feebly attempted classes at the community college.

I used any scholarship money I had left over to buy coke and party with my friends from my old college. Often I would just disappear for days, not answering my phone, sleeping on friends' couches and terrifying my family until I would come crawling home. There were periods where I would attempt to pull it together. I got a decent job at a catering company in Nashville, which also gave me more opportunity for getting away from home and getting drunk. I remember partying one night and freaking out the next day because I couldn't find my shoes for work. My friends and I found them in the middle of the road.

I met Big Mike at that job. He was tall and strong, loud and smart. A handsome, authoritative figure in his chef uniform, he was twenty-eight and going through a divorce. I was twenty, and I guess my mess was hidden enough at work that he took an interest in me. He had a house and an education. He was working on his master's degree. I lived in unending delusion that this guy would rescue me, that if I could be good enough, he would love me and all my sins would be absolved. My past would be forgiven, and I would be vindicated and seen.

I was anxious every day, filled with an overwhelming need for attention, which sometimes he gave and sometimes he didn't. I know now that I loved the roller coaster and pain. He would get furious with me if I came over drunk, so I tried to hide it. I needed to be drunk to have sex with him, so it was always a tightrope walk, a juggling act, a shit-show circus, trying to find the balance of how much I could drink before he would get frustrated but drunk enough so I could give him what I thought he wanted. I changed how I dressed, I stopped hanging out with hippies. I mostly quit doing drugs. I tried to be what he wanted, but my relationship with him was so painful, I used alcohol to numb myself and perpetuate my delusion.

I eventually changed jobs and became a full-time server. Working in restaurants was a perfect fit for my lifestyle. I made decent money, and all the people I worked with were like a dysfunctional family who condoned all my favorite, twisted behaviors. We'd make a pile of cash and then be rubbed so raw by our day or night of work we would hit the bar with serious intent. Our manager loved to party as well. He'd get drunk and hit on the girls. I spent a Sunday afternoon doing blow with him and another young girl, getting out of our minds and out of our clothes. There was always some guy I worked with available to help me harm myself with alcohol and sex. This was when I started to feel the need to drink in the mornings or afternoons, between shifts, to ease exhaustion or numb hangovers.

I was still living at home during this time, and Mike had moved nearby. A distance had developed between us, but I was still so attached to the idea of him. He picked me up one night and we slept together. I was kind of drunk, of course. On the drive home the next day, I told him about how I was in therapy and trying to get better. As he dropped me off, he told me it was a good idea and to keep trying. He called me that night to tell me he was dating someone. I was destroyed and tore into a liter of vodka with ferocity. I stayed drunk for a solid couple of days.

The next week, I showed up wasted to work and got sent home. A friend let me come over and fed me a few painkillers and some booze and I slept for a long, long time. My therapist convinced me it was time for rehab. I decided I would give it a shot, knowing that I couldn't live with all the pain anymore. The scariest part for me was sitting my parents down and telling them I needed to go, and that I needed a ride there. As my mom dropped me off, I remember trying to comfort her. It'll be okay, Mom. I just wanted to get better so I could make it all better and be loved.

In rehab, I was a good camper. I did what they said, tried to be honest about my feelings, behaved myself. They bused us to AA meetings. I ate salad and played volleyball. I would do what they said and I would get fixed. They recommended I move to a halfway house when I left treatment, so I did. I felt so lost and alone and lasted only a few weeks before I moved home.

My mom came to help me move my things. On the way home, I took a different route so I could stop and buy a bottle. It felt like someone else was driving the car. I could absolutely separate myself from the moment and move outside of my body in order to deny the truth and get what I needed to escape consciousness.

I got another restaurant job and started increasing my skills at functioning drunk on a daily basis. I brought bottles to work, hid beers in the bathroom. Stole booze from the bar. I got caught several times, but for reasons I still don't understand, I didn't get fired from that job. I found more men to degrade me and reinforce my self-hatred. I'd wake up in dilapidated houses on a dirty mattress, or hiding in the apartment above a tattoo shop with some man old enough to be my dad. My parents would always look for me, my younger siblings getting accustomed to my insane behavior. No one trusted me; everyone was tired of my tears and pathetic excuses. They would get so angry with me, and I could never get them to understand that there was no one more angry at me than ME. I was my greatest judge. I punished myself more than anyone ever could. Total destruction is what I wanted and deserved.

Chris started working at my restaurant. He was older and cute and had great taste in music. I wanted his attention. I came on to him. He had his own struggles with alcohol. I was drunk the first time we hung out, and I never changed that. I started staying over a lot. I had a place to drink, someone to ease my loneliness. I was taking a lot of Xanax during this time. One morning, still drunk from the night before, I started drinking and took some pills. I decided to clean and do laundry for Chris. I think I blacked out or passed out for a second while driving and rear-ended someone. Again.

Being in my hometown, the arresting officer was a guy whose wedding I had been in. This was all just more stuff I could use against myself to confirm what horrible person I knew I was. I couldn't face my parents, and Chris let me move in immediately. I stayed with him for three years. Putting him through all the ups and downs of my drinking. Trying to quit, not being able to. I'd drink so much that sometimes I'd wet our bed. He never got angry with me. I tried my best to love him, but there was nothing inside me to really give. He took care of me and fed me. I would have brief periods of sobriety when things would be bright and fun. Then I would just go so deep into my shame and pain and pursuit of nonexistence. I clung to him and used him to help me survive and stay drunk.

A year after my DUI I was finally sentenced to five days in jail, much better than the forty-five I was supposed to serve. I detoxed a bit, and the relief was amazing. I decided to return to my therapist and try to start over. I got my own apartment and tried to get healthy and normal. It took several months, but eventually I started losing my urge to drink to excess. My therapist started helping me face my sexual trauma and my anger toward my parents, who were going through a messy divorce.

Using Eye Movement Desensitization and Reprocessing, I learned a little bit about sitting with the emotional pain of my experiences, and knowing that I was okay. It was amazing to be able to speak the truth about things that had happened in my family. I quit drinking, started exercising. I enrolled in a Spanish class and excelled. I started liking myself just a little bit. I was finally taking care of myself. I lost a ton of weight and felt good. I started finding out little things, like what colors I liked. Trying to connect with myself.

I stopped having sex with Chris and slowly let go of that relationship. I knew I needed to end it, but I felt so guilty and dependent on him to be okay on my own. My actions weren't fair to him, but I didn't know how else to extract myself. It was all so new. I felt closer to my family and finally able to be there for my little brother and sister.

The hardest part was finding people in that small town I could connect with. I didn't have many people I could relate to and always felt like I was trying to make up for my reputation. I met my friend Celia, a loving, beautiful world traveler, who led a life that inspired me. She invited me to move to Mexico with her. I decided to do it. I thought I could do it and stay sober, but shortly before I left, I decided I could manage drinking again. After a few months of tasting life how I wanted it to be, I went back to alcohol. Nothing disastrous happened. I upset my family, but I was able to manage things. I turned twenty-five, gave up my apartment, left my job, broke up with Chris, packed my bag, and headed to the mountains in Mexico.

Mexico was amazing, but it was a place where I could feed my addiction without fear. My skills as a drunk showed up for me, and I immediately found men to lean on. I knew inside that I was depriving myself of something, that I was missing out on the greater part of this experience, but I couldn't really stop myself. I didn't want to. It felt great to have my ability to party accepted, to seek out nothing but fun.

I came home drunk and broke. I had to move back in with my mom. As Celia got her things in order so she could move back to Mexico long term, I was stuck again. I went back to my old restaurant. I slept on my mom's couch, reexhibiting all the behaviors that had gone on for years.

I eventually made my way out of town, to Nashville. I started new jobs where my drinking would immediately interfere and I would get fired. I was broker than I ever was in my life. I truly didn't recognize myself in the mirror. My face was always swollen and red. My skin was horrible, I had thinning hair, and I was overweight again despite how little I actually ate. My mouth was always raw from dehydration and from drinking Taaka right out of the bottle.

I put myself in more dangerous situations, waking up in strange beds with strange men, driving drunk again. I thought about death so much that it scared me. I met another older guy who provided me with booze and sex and food. My body started to have trouble with all the abuse, and a urinary tract infection turned into a kidney infection overnight. I was drinking and pissing blood. I went to the ER and they gave me antibiotics and pain meds. I kept drinking.

I went home for Christmas, drunk as hell, stopping only to pick up a forty-ounce. My little brother received a nice bottle of whiskey for Christmas. I drank it with a handful of pills. A sloppy, crying, thieving disaster on Christmas. My little sister looked at me and told me she was done with me.

I had no money, and I was about to get fired again. I could hardly function anymore. I left my mom's house after Christmas, desperate to not drink. I didn't want to go to rehab again, but I knew I had to change something. I bought a beer on the way home. I remember sipping it as I looked at my ER bill. I got a bottle of wine after work. I remember being too tired to drink much, but knew I couldn't sleep without it. The pain that entered my body whenever I quit drinking was terrifying. My heart felt like it would explode. I truly didn't want to do this to myself anymore. I really, really wanted to learn to live.

I ran into an old friend who invited me for coffee. He seemed different and happier than I remembered him. I clutched at the table in the coffee shop, trying to hang on as I told him I was desperate to change my life. I was scared and afraid of death and I didn't want to drink anymore. I told him how I felt that rehab and AA weren't the answer for me. He told me about this meditation group he was going to. He told me that it definitely wasn't a cult and that I should give it a try.

I showed up to my first meditation feeling pretty blank. I had managed to not drink for a couple weeks and had even started sleeping a little. The first sit was not as hard as I thought. I felt like I could do this. The people seemed all right. I kept going. I never wanted to talk to anyone; I just came and left. I was afraid of being a part of something that reminded me of church.

I tried sitting a bit on my own, using guided meditations. Eating became a part of my life again. With time, so did sleeping. Everything slowed down. There was less terror in my head. I began to connect with people in the meditation group, forming some tentative friendships. I didn't really know if the actual meditation stuff was helping, or if it was just me hanging on.

I heard a lot of things talked about that I had never heard of before; mindfulness practice and Buddhism were totally foreign to me. I read *Dharma Punx*. I got a Thich Nhat Hanh book, so I could try to understand what the hell people were saying. What I did grasp was that it was okay for me to simply be at any stage of practice. I didn't have to feel bad or beat myself up. A gentle turning down of the volume of my self-hatred. The phrase that spoke to me so deeply during the guided sits was "You can't do this wrong." Maybe I was too tired to turn away from everything. So I just did it. And it helped. I learned that I could sit in my pain, and it wouldn't kill me. That the moment is here, and it is like this.

A couple months into my sobriety I got incredibly sick. Flu rocked my body. I would wake up three or four times in the night to change my clothes, which were soaked through with sweat. My body ached, my kidneys ached. I lay on the couch where I had done so much drunk time and let my body rattle out the last gasps of detox. It was terrifying, exhausting, and incredibly painful.

A girl from the meditation group brought me some soup. Just that simple act blew me away. Accepting the help was hard for me, but there was something about that soup that helped me know I wasn't alone anymore, not if I didn't want to be.

Gradually, as my body healed and my mind cleared, the basic concepts of the Dharma started to resonate with me. With time, I began to learn the Dharma points to the inherent suffering in life, but that I can still learn to be with it. My sits became painful at times. I signed up for a class with our teacher and was introduced to the heart practices. Loving-kindness, forgiveness, compassion, appreciative joy, equanimity. These helped me face and carry the things that hurt. I turned toward all my pain, anger, confusion, and despair, learning to care about these things instead of pushing it all away and wallowing in my desire for things to be different. Meeting my pain with loving-kindness seemed to give me a foundation to stand on.

Instead of just desperately clinging to each moment of sobriety and trying to not drink, I began to learn how to be with pain and joy and be okay. Meditation cut right into my core and addressed my heart. I've begun to see my craving as part of my humanity, not something that is wrong with me. I no longer feel as though I need to be "fixed." Meditation helps me see how I crave all things pleasurable and absolutely hate what is uncomfortable, but it also helps me see the truth of impermanence. What I hate and am uncomfortable with right now will pass, and what is pleasurable and joyous will also pass. There are times when this is a great comfort to me, and times when it really hurts.

Things in my life began to transform. My roommate moved out, and Celia came home from Mexico and moved in. My sister got out of our small hometown and joined us. My house went from a place where all I knew was desperation and loneliness to a place of safety and love. It was the warmest spring of my life. It was difficult to go from practically living alone to having all these people in my life, but I knew it was good for me despite my frustrations. I learned about compromise and sharing; I learned to let go a little more.

One morning, as I was driving to the park, a lady ran a red light and totaled my car. This was the first time I noticed a change had taken place. Months before, this would have been a perfect opportunity to freak out and play the victim, to feel desperate and terrified, to angrily shake my fist at life. Instead, I felt grateful that for the first time I was not at fault in an accident, that the police officer wasn't going to take me to jail. I had a driver's license, insurance. No one was hurt. I was shocked at how at ease I was with this happening. I was broke and without a car, but I knew I'd be okay. A drastic difference from my attitude just months before. My sister even commented, "Man, this Dharma stuff seems to really work."

Nine months into meditation practice and sobriety, I went on a weeklong silent meditation retreat in Yucca Valley, followed by a solo Amtrak trip up the coast to Seattle, then to Chicago before hitting Memphis and coming back to Nashville. The retreat was an excellent opportunity for me to find that I had developed faith, and to deepen my meditation practice by having direct instructions by teachers. I was continuously confronted by fear that I had become a part of some cult, that this was just more religious bullshit. What I found is that the outward forms don't really matter much to me. My direct experiences with meditation and practice were the most important thing. I have seen my inner dialogue change, and my ability to love myself and others grow as a direct result of the Dharma. I can practice anywhere, whether I am in the desert, on a cushion, or riding the bus.

Mostly, though, what I felt was overwhelming gratitude for the ways my life had changed, for the fact that I could sit still with myself for so long, that I had at least the willingness to put forth this effort to change in my life. Early recovery made the experience overwhelmingly beautiful for me. Afterward, riding that train up the coast was one of the greatest gifts I've ever given myself. Feeling the smallness as well as the importance of my place in this world. For so long, I thought that all I wanted was to be loved, and the Dharma helped me find all the love inside myself.

This has been the most important part of my personal practice, love as something I cultivate within and not something I desperately search for. I have forgiven myself for the past. My relationships with men have transformed. I can hold myself with love and self-respect, and men in my Sangha have taught me about healthy emotional intimacy and friendship, and I have learned about my value as a woman beyond sex. The paradigm of my desires has changed, and I am learning about being my own hero rather than looking for someone to rescue me.

Shortly after I returned home from traveling, I shattered my knee on a trampoline. I never knew anything could hurt so bad. Unable to afford insurance, I knew I was screwed. I was terrified about having to go to the hospital, and even more scared about being given painkillers. I've never experienced that kind of pain or fear. The situation was completely out of my control, one of the worst things I could imagine. I'd never been physically incapacitated, and it was excruciating; nothing terrified me more than not being able to take care of myself. The news from the doctors kept getting worse. They said it would be months before I could walk again. I have always struggled with asking for help, and this had put me in a position of extreme need.

My practice showed up for me. The only way I could find ease in that situation was to be in each moment. As soon as I would worry about the future or what would happen to me, I would mentally spiral out of control. ALL I could do was breathe into the moment and find faith. The pain made painkillers necessary for a brief time, and I was afraid of relapse. My sister helped me keep track of what I was taking, but for the most part it was up to me. I saw that I had a choice. I could take this experience and grow and know the pain and know my fear, or I could check out and wake up a few months later with just nothing but months of being doped up in front of the TV behind me. I didn't want that.

Just moving from the couch to the bathroom was an overwhelming task. For months, I was reliant on the help of others and continuously surprised at how readily available people were. Having lived in so much self-hatred and with such strong beliefs that I never deserved to be loved, this became one of the greatest experiences of my life. For months, people brought food, came to visit. People gave me money. My faith in the moment was deepened immeasurably. I learned to be less afraid of pain, less afraid of the future. I was forced to sit and look at the richness of my life. To see how different things had become since I got sober. I celebrated a year of sobriety steeped in love and gratitude.

Now over a year into my practice, I never knew that life could be like this. As I get used to walking again, and being back in the world, I find that my faith in myself and in the Dharma has deepened. There are times when I feel as though things are static and I question and doubt my practice. But I find that with effort I am able to continue my path. Without the drugs, alcohol, and harmful sex, the meditation continues to open my eyes to new ways in which I can become free. Mental and emotional habits have started to change. Not only has the angry judge in my mind become quieter, I have learned I don't have to listen to the endless rants of self-judgment or self-hatred.

Forgiveness, kindness, and compassion have become an ongoing process in my life, and I am not seeking a magical point of arrival when I will finally be done hurting or learning. My heart has melted into a tender and supple muscle that beats passionately, even when it feels broken. I have learned about trust and support, connection, and openness through Sangha. I don't feel as though I have subscribed to a set of beliefs, like a religion, but that I have picked up a valuable set of tools that I utilize daily. Dharma has become something that lives and breathes in my life, influencing and changing my perspective continuously. Inclusive and fluid, I don't find that it prescribes guilt or regret when I make mistakes. It allows me to open my view and learn a better way to live. I didn't find a cure for my pain or past, but a path that seems to always lead me toward more freedom and authenticity in my life.

22

Andrea

I was born perfect. When I look at pictures of that tiny face and hopeful eyes, something I was taught to do by a Dharma teacher, I understand there's nothing wrong with me. Nothing ever was; nothing ever will be. Anything that happened before I came of age is not my fault. At the same time, everything about me is my responsibility. Recovery is full of paradoxes. I was born perfect and I'm totally fucked up. It's not my fault and it's totally my responsibility. Alcoholism and addiction are diseases I might never fully recover from, but I can be free of drugs, alcohol, starving, and overeating, for as long as I take refuge in my own recovery and stay close to the people who help me on the path of physical and emotional sobriety.

I started drinking when I was nine, but the circumstances leading up to that first vodka and orange juice I gulped along with my Cocoa Puffs before I went off to fourth grade began long before. My mom was beautiful. She was an artist. She was also mentally ill when my father married her. Undiagnosed and self-medicated, she left for a year when I was four months old. I don't remember that abandonment, but apparently my body does. When I was four, she tried to kill herself with me in the house. Four may not be my lucky number. I never wanted to talk about these things, or anything in my past, because it made me feel "poor me" and being a victim disgusted me. I picked vodka for my first drink because that's what my mom liked. Mom had just announced to my older sister and me that she wasn't coming down to make us breakfast anymore, that my sister was a miserable kid, and that we were on our own. My sister's eyes brightened. "We can have pie for breakfast!" she said. I was filled with hopeless despair and longing and rummaged for the vodka so I could feel close to my mom, although for her alcohol was just to make the opiates kick in harder.

Living a double life is what I remember most about childhood. There was the girl I was at school, popular and smart, already the "all A" kid. I called that girl "puppet me," because that's what I felt like inside. The real me was a girl so lonely at home, already lying to her friends about my mom and embarrassed to have anyone come over because of the syringes lying around from my mom shooting Demerol, and scarier still, my drug-addled, unkempt, rage-filled mother.

My dad was a doctor. He spent most days taking care of people he could actually help. But he was also the source of my mother's drugs. I called him a lot to come home from the hospital where he worked whenever I found my mom passed out on the floor, having fallen out of bed. I did this until the day he told me, "She's all right," and didn't come right home. Then, I moved out. I was fourteen. I moved in with my best girlfriend's family and wished I had thought of it sooner.

Life at my best friend's house was free of alcohol, and her parents were kind, except for one little issue I buried entirely in sobriety. Since I was nine her father had lain on top of me, kissing me and rubbing himself against me whenever I visited her house. Moving in made for easier access until her parents got divorced, but by then I was a fixture in their family, and I went with my friend and her sisters to their father's house on weekends. I honestly didn't know this was sexual abuse. I thought he was my boyfriend. I had to be told in sobriety to stop calling him my first boyfriend. It lasted until I skipped twelfth grade and went to college. I needed somebody's arms around me and was okay that they were his.

Sobriety came to me unplanned, with the same random intensity that everything else I experienced did. I was with my teenage boyfriend at the doctor getting birth control. I would never have thought to take care of myself in that way or any other. The doctor asked standard questions about my drug and alcohol use. I didn't think to lie about the combination of Xanax and alcohol I was consuming because I had already given up cocaine six months earlier on my own. The doctor looked at me and said, "You're going to die. You're going to go into a coma and not wake up, or do it behind the wheel of a car and take other people with you. I don't want you as my patient." Huh? I didn't know doctors could fire people. I walked out to the waiting room and told my nonaddict boyfriend what she had said. I went to AA the very next day. I can't say it was because I didn't want to die. I had taken my mom's Seconals many times, looked in the mirror, and said, "Wake me when I die," but something about the doctor's open contempt and accusation didn't jibe with "little Andi with the heart of gold," the name I was called all through childhood.

I'm twenty-seven years sober, though I didn't find my way to Dharma until five years ago. I got sober first try. I didn't like alcohol much. Like my mom, it was just to make the pills work quicker, and in my case, as a substitute for giving up coke. So many other tools got and kept me sober. One way or the other, I had to take the first step—admitting I was powerless over alcohol and drugs. Alcoholics Anonymous worked really well for that, as well as the 12-step fellowship of people my own age, all of whom were struggling with the same life and physical issues. The specificity of the 12-step world, however, troubled me. Addicts are rarely allowed to talk about one addiction in the rooms of another addiction, which confused the hell out of cross-addicted me. Yes, I was sober, but sober isn't sane. My body didn't like being here. Reality felt much too harsh. Before I had my first year sober, I had become anorexic, going down to 109 pounds at five feet, nine inches tall. This time, it was Gabrielle Roth, an extraordinary dance teacher, who saved me. She introduced me to a spiritual movement practice called "the 5 Rhythms." She encouraged me and her other students to dance until we shattered ourselves, till we disappeared and only the dance remained. Gabrielle wanted us all to smash the ego, the false self, the one with the mind of its own that urges us to believe everything it tells us, and everything it tells us is awful. Dancing the 5 Rhythms was my first attempt at being in my body, at really inhabiting this thing I had been trying to get away from since that morning of unbearable pain when my mom wanted to get away from my sister and me. I poured myself into dance, and instead of getting more grounded, I fluttered away even further, sometimes for six or eight hours a day. And this is who I was—sober, but not fully here, running from sadness again, only this time with some really awesome music.

My heart eventually led me to Dharma at Against the Stream in Santa Monica, where Noah, the ex-addict with tats on his neck and love in his heart, seemed to be living what he was teaching. So did the other teachers he trained. Plus, there were enough guys with spiderweb tattoos on their elbows to keep me interested until the cushion did. I didn't have to be a Buddhist, Noah said. "Be a Buddha instead." He also challenged my obsession with dance, asking what I thought would happen if I actually sat down. I liked the idea of ending suffering but didn't think it was possible. Certainly not by spending more time with sadness. Nonattachment, nonclinging? Anyone who said they could love without putting a

net over the other person's head so he or she didn't go away didn't
have my mom. And loving-kindness toward myself? It just wasn't
doable.

But here's the thing. Just like the 12 steps and dance, if I take
refuge in the Dharma, the Dharma embraces me. Truth telling, the
one without words that happens in the silence and in the precepts
of nonharm and nonviolence, works like a balm on the soul. Some
of us get lucky early. "Putting the plug in the jug" is enough. If
alcohol is the problem, and we don't drink the alcohol, problem
solved. But for people like me, where taking away the anesthesia
leaves me bleeding without relief, something older, wiser, and time
tested over thousands of years promises I can get free. And from
the first time I tried Buddhism in Refuge Recovery until my last
Dharma talk yesterday, I've received the same encouragement I
now offer: "These are my thoughts. Investigate them, try them out,
and see what's true for you."

Appendixes

Meditation is the cornerstone of our path. Here are a number of guided meditation instructions to get you started. Also seek out wise guidance from qualified Buddhist meditation teachers.

Mindfulness Meditation Instructions

1. The Body

Part 1: Breathing

Find a comfortable place to sit. Adjust your posture so that your spine is erect without being rigid or stiff. Allow the rest of your body to be relaxed around the upright spine. Rest your hands in your lap or on your legs. Allow your eyes to gently close. Bring full attention to the physical sensations of sitting still. Allow your breathing to be natural. Bringing attention to your head, release any tension in the face, soften the eyes, and relax the jaw. Scanning the body slowly downward, relax the neck and shoulders. Feeling the rise and fall of the chest and abdomen with the breath, soften the belly with each exhalation. Bringing the attention all the way down through the body to the places of contact with the chair or cushion, allow your body to be supported by the seat you're on. Feel the pressure and density of the relaxed upright body sitting.

Bringing your full attention to the present-time experience, acknowledge the full range of phenomena that are happening in the moment. Thinking is happening; hearing is happening; seeing (even with the eyes closed), tasting, smelling, and physical and emotional sensations are all present. Allowing all the experiences to be as they are, redirect your attention to the sensations of the breath. Let the other sense experiences fall to the background as you bring the awareness of breathing to the foreground. Take a few moments to investigate where you feel the breath most easily (usually either at the base of the nostrils or in the rising and falling of the abdomen). Find the place where you feel the breath coming and going, and use that as the point of focus. (Choose one place and stick with it; don't jump back and forth between nose and belly. It is not necessary to follow the breath in and out.)

Breathing in, *know* that you are breathing in. Breathing out, *know* that you are breathing out. A simple way to stay focused is by quietly acknowledging in your mind, *in* on the inhalation and *out* on the exhalation (if you are paying attention at the nostrils), or rising and falling (if you are paying attention at the abdomen). Another skillful technique is to count the breath. Breathing in, one; out, two; in, three; out, four. Try to get to ten. And then begin to count back down to one.

Of course, you will quickly realize that your attention will not stay with the breath; the attention will be drawn back into thinking over and over. In the beginning, the practice of meditation is often just the practice of training the attention to return to the breath. Each time the attention wanders back to the thinking aspect of the mind, gently redirect it back to the breath. (This natural process of training the mind is the essence of meditation.)

It is important to understand that this will happen over and over. It doesn't mean that you are doing anything wrong or that you can't meditate. It just means that you, like all people, are so used to *thinking* about things rather than *feeling* them that the attention is naturally drawn into thinking again and again. Until you have trained the attention to connect and sustain contact with the sensory experience rather than the mental experience, your practice is just that, training the attention in what we call present-time awareness.

Bring the attention back to the simple experience of the breath over and over. Breathing in, know that the breath is coming into the body. Breathing out, know that the breath is leaving the body. Each time the attention wanders into thinking or to another sense experience, acknowledge that that has happened, noting the thinking or hearing or seeing, and then again return the attention to the awareness of the breath. Start over at one each time the attention wanders. Come back again and again. When you can sustain breath awareness for about ten minutes, you are ready to expand to the next foundations.

While you are training the mind in present-time awareness of the breath, with the mind's almost constant wandering and returning, it is important to bring a quality of kindness and understanding to the practice. Try to be friendly toward your experience. Of course the attention wanders. Try not to take it personally; it's not your fault. That's just what the untrained mind does. It will take some time and perseverance to train the attention to stay with the chosen object of awareness. It is necessary to be patient and kind to yourself in the process.

Easier said than done. But when you get caught (judging yourself, being too critical, or doubting the process), attempt to bring a friendliness to your relationship to the thoughts. And then simply redirect the attention back to the breath.

Part 2: The Breath and Body

Begin the same way you did in the first meditation, finding a comfortable place to sit, closing the eyes, and relaxing the body.

Bringing attention to the sensations of breath, continue redirecting the attention to the breath each time it wanders. Continue to be as friendly and kind as possible to your mind's tendency to wander.

After about ten minutes of focusing the attention on the breath, begin to expand the attention to the whole body. Bring attention to your posture. Feel the pressure of your body on the cushion or chair. Feel the contact points of your hands touching your legs or resting in your lap. Direct the attention to sensations in the body of sitting.

With the foundation of present-time awareness, as established by the continual returning of the attention to the breath and body, you can now allow the attention to expand to include all of the sense doors.

Begin with the awareness of hearing. When you become aware of a sound, simply pay attention to the experience of hearing—the bare experience of sound being received by the eardrum. Although the mind wants to instantly name the object being heard, the direct experience is just variations of sound. Using memory and conditioning, the mind immediately tries to label the sound as a car passing by, or the wind in the trees, or the refrigerator turning on. In this level of practice, try to see the difference between the direct experience of sound and the mind's conditioned labeling of the experience. Keep it simple; it is just hearing.

Expand your attention to seeing, tasting, and smelling in the same way. Just seeing and the direct experience of what's being seen—color, shape, form, and so on. Just taste. Just smelling.

Notice how quickly the mind names and classifies things based on memory. This level of mindfulness allows us to see how the mind is constantly trying to sort and name experiences based on memory, rarely allowing for new or fresh perspectives.

When the attention gets drawn back into thinking, simply return it to the breath. Then continue to extend mindfulness to the direct, moment-to-moment sensory experience of the whole body.

Allow the attention to be drawn to whatever experience in the body is predominant. When sounds arise, know them as hearing. When visions arise, know them as seeing. Don't settle for the mind's labels and conventions. Experience each moment as if it were the first sensation of its kind ever. Bring childlike interest and curiosity to your present-time experience. What does this moment feel like? What is the temperature, texture, or pressure of this sensory experience?

Continue to connect the attention with the felt sense of the breath and body. Begin refining the attention to the moment-to-moment flux of sensations. Investigate the constantly changing nature of each experience.

With clear comprehension, receive the transient phenomena with nonjudgmental awareness. Attempt to sustain awareness of the arising and passing of each chosen sensation.

Continue redirecting the attention and reconnecting with the present moment each time the attention is drawn back into the contents of the thinking mind.

Attempt to rest in the direct experience of the breath and body, relaxing into the present-time awareness of impermanence.

Part 3: Parts of the Body

As you continue to direct mindfulness to the present-time experience, the next level of practice is to bring attention to the different parts of the body. Start at the top of your head. Bring attention to the crown of your skull, hair, and scalp. Then slowly scan your attention downward visualizing and taking inventory of all the parts of your body. Forehead, eyebrows, eyelids, eyes, nose, cheeks, ears, jaw, lips, mouth, teeth, tongue, chin. Feel your face, and all its parts. Include the muscles, tendons, arteries, and veins. Visualize your brain resting in the cradle of your skull. Your inner eardrum. How the nose and throat connect. Taste buds, smell receptors. The gelatinous nature of your eyeballs.

Begin to scan the attention down the neck. Visualize your throat, the passageways leading to the stomach and lungs. Vocal cords. Muscles, veins, arteries. Vertebrae. This is what holds your head on to your body. Feel it.

Scan your attention down into the trunk of your body. Clavicles, shoulders, chest, upper back. Skin, bones, joints, muscles, veins and arteries. Breasts, nipples, ribs, sternum, vertebrae, and organs.

Before continuing the investigation of the midsection, bring the attention down the arms. Biceps, triceps, elbow, forearm, wrist, and hands. Without moving your hands feel your fingers, fingernails, palms.

Now, return to the trunk of the body. Take inventory. Heart, lungs, liver, spleen, stomach, kidneys, gallbladder, intestines, reproductive organs, colon, bladder. Fat, feces, and urine. Visualize the trunk of your body, as if the skin was removed and you could see all your inner workings. The rib cage protecting the lungs and heart. The vertebrae allowing you to be upright, to sit, to stand, and also to bend.

Continue to scan down, into the buttocks and genitalia. Penis and testicles or vagina. The anus. Skin, hair, muscles, arteries and veins. The pelvis.

Next are the thighs. This is the largest muscle, the largest artery, and the largest bone in the body. Visualize your femur. And how it connects to the pelvis and the knee.

Then bring attention down into the knees. Kneecap, back of the knee, connecting to lower leg. Calves, shins, and ankles.

Finally the feet. Heels, arch, top of the foot, and toes. Toenails. Bones, joints, skin, hair.

Having scanned the attention through the body, we reflect on the impermanence of this body that is subject to sickness, injury, aging, and death. We also reflect on all the unpleasant smells and sensations that come with having a body. This is what we are identified with and what we are often lusting after, a body that is filled with blood, feces, and urine.

Be mindful of the true nature of the body.

Part 4: Four Elements

As we direct mindfulness to the body, we begin to understand that all that is being experienced here, in the body, are the four elements. With each breath, we experience the air element. Warmth or coolness in the body directs us to the experience of the fire element. Saliva in the mouth, blinking of the eyes, and beating of the heart are the water element. And the contact with the chair, cushion, or footstep draws our attention to the earth element. This body, when investigated, shows us that the skeleton is earth, and the skeleton is surrounded by water-based muscles and organs. The muscles and organs are warm; we have a natural fire inside. And the body is a porous, breathing organism. Not only is air entering and exiting through the nose and mouth. The skin itself is constantly breathing.

Sit in meditation and observe closely all aspects of this body. Name what element you are being mindful of in each moment. See if you can find any part of the body that is not of the four elements.

Perhaps you will speculate about the experience of thought or emotion being nonmaterial. And although from one perspective this is true, it is through the four elements that we have a brain and heart to give rise to thoughts and emotions, so technically, they are part of the four elements too. This is what it is like when all four elements come together in the form of a living human body. The body experiences emotions, the mind experiences thoughts, and they both experience pleasure and pain.

Part 5: Corpse/Death Meditation

Sitting or lying down in a comfortable place, allow your eyes to close, and relax into the present-time experience. Feel your breath as it comes and goes. Notice the heaviness of the physical body, the pressure against the cushion or floor. Feel the effects of gravity on your body.

Begin to imagine or visualize your body as a corpse. See your body as motionless and inanimate. Acknowledge that this is the inevitable destiny of the body, and breathe in and out of the place of acceptance of death.

Now begin to see your body as dead for several days, bloated and beginning to rot. Imagine your body as lifeless and in an advanced stage of decomposition. Allow your imagination to be as graphic as you'd like—worms eating your flesh, maggots, and so on.

Then move on to seeing your body as a skeleton, all the flesh and blood gone, bones and ligaments alone remaining. Even the bones are beginning to crumble, eventually falling apart and scattering until finally only dust remains.

After some time, allow the reflection to end and return to mindfulness of your breath and body in the present moment.

(This meditation is meant to bring appreciation and preciousness to life. By acknowledging death and decay, we remember the importance of each moment of life.)

2. Feeling Tone

After establishing some ability to sustain attention, you can begin to investigate the "feeling tone" of each experience. Whether you are paying attention to the breath or sensations in the body, each experience has a feeling tone of pleasantness, unpleasantness, or neutrality. By focusing the attention a little bit more and opening your awareness to the subtle levels of pleasant and unpleasant tones of experience, you bring mindfulness to your craving for pleasure and aversion to pain. Feeling tone is the place where one gets attached or aversive.

Begin by practicing the first two meditations. Always begin sitting meditation by focusing on the present-time experience of the body. This allows the attention to settle in the here and now. As a basic guideline, ten to twenty minutes of breath/body awareness is a good idea before expanding to this next level of practice. (The amount of time depends on one's ability to concentrate.)

While sitting with awareness focused on the body, refine the attention to the feeling tone of your experience. Investigate and inquire into the nature of the experience you are paying attention to. Is this a pleasant feeling? Does it feel good? Or is it an uncomfortable experience. Are you resisting the present feeling? Bring mindfulness to the feeling itself; see for yourself how you relate to pleasure and pain.

What does your mind do when the present-time experience is neutral? Are you able to hang out with experiences that have no pleasure or pain associated with them? Or does the mind get bored and seek a pleasurable or painful memory or plan?

Continue training the mind in this way. Each time the attention wanders, gently return to the present moment and continue investigating your inner relationship to the pleasant, unpleasant, or neutral tone of each moment.

When you become aware of attachment to a pleasurable experience, attempt to let go. Release the mind/body's grip by softening and relaxing into each moment. Experience fully the pleasure as it comes and goes.

When you become aware of aversion to an unpleasant experience, attempt to meet it with mercy and friendliness. Allow the pain or discomfort to be present, and meet it with the understanding that it will pass if you just allow it to come through the mind/body without trying to resist it, suppress it, or control it.

When you are meditating on neutral phenomena, attempt to relax into the absence of suffering. Tolerate the mind's craving for pleasure and continue to enjoy the experience of just being. Learning to enjoy the absence of pleasure and pain is key on the meditative path.

3. The Mind

Part 1: Process

From the foundation of present-time investigative awareness that is infused with the intention of kindness and understanding, you can turn your attention on the mind itself.

After having established awareness of the breath/body and the feeling tone of the present moment, expand the attention to the process of the thinking mind. Observe the arising and passing of thoughts. Allow the awareness to be expansive: try not to get caught in the content of the thoughts; let go of the need to solve any problems or make any plans. Just relax into the present-time awareness of thoughts coming and going.

Break the addiction to the contents of and identification with your mind. Meditate on the mind as a process. Each thought is like a bubble floating through the spaciousness of awareness. One may contain a plan, another a memory, and yet another a judgment or an emotion. Allow each thought to pass without getting into the bubble or floating off with it.

Until the meditation practice has matured, you will get seduced by the thinking mind over and over, floating off into a plan or memory that feels too important to let pass. Or all of a sudden you will have what seems like the most important revelation or inspiration. This is the natural process of training the mind and transforming your relationship to the contents of your mind. As with the breath, simply let go and return to the present over and over, bursting the bubble and redirecting the attention to the process again and again.

If there is a foundation of attention that is concentrated and stable, you may be able to experience the completely impersonal phenomenon of the proliferation of thoughts. You may see that one thought that arises leads to the next and the next and the next, until suddenly the mind is off in some fantasy, each bubble giving birth to the next.

Part 2: Content

After establishing awareness of the breath/body and feeling tone of the present moment, and after expanding the attention to the process of the thinking mind and observing the arising and passing of thoughts, bring attention to the contents of each mind moment. Know directly the truth of each thought. Be aware of each memory as a memory, and when a plan arises in the mind, know it as a plan—perhaps noting "past" and "future."

Be aware of the arising of all emotion. If fear, anger, sadness, love, caring, envy, empathy, or any other feeling arises, experience it directly; know that it originated in the mind and has manifested in the body as well. You may see that fear is an underlying motivator for much of the contents of the mind. See for yourself what is true about your mind.

Know each experience as it is. Observe the tendency to avoid, suppress, ignore, or resist the unpleasant thoughts, and recognize that as aversion. Observe the tendency to cling, crave, and feed the thoughts that are pleasant or that you feel will lead to more safety or happiness, and know that experience as attachment. And then let go, let go, let go.

4. The Truth

The fourth level of mindfulness meditation is bringing awareness to the truth of the present moment. Through the introspective practice of present-time awareness we can bring attention to the truth of suffering, its causes, and the experience of freedom from suffering and confusion. At this level, we can pay attention to and know when suffering is present, when craving has arisen, and when contentment and peace are being experienced. This level of mindfulness extends to all the experiences we have. Traditionally this includes the awareness of the arising and passing of the hindrances, the senses, the noble truths, the factors of enlightenment, and the attachments and cravings that keep us ignorant about the truths of existence.

While sitting in meditation, expand the attention to the whole mind and body. Know your experience as it is. When you become aware of the hindrances of sleepiness, restlessness, craving, aversion, or doubt, simply pay direct attention to the truth of these experiences. What does it feel like in the body? Where do you physically experience restlessness, sleepiness, aversion, or craving? Is the experience constant or constantly changing?

Likewise with the factors of awakening: when mindfulness, concentration, investigation, energy, joy, equanimity, and relaxation arise, take them as the object of meditation. Investigate and contemplate the truth of each moment as it manifests in the body and mind.

On this level of meditative practice it is important to keep the intention of objective friendliness. Meet each experience with acceptance and curiosity: "So this is suffering; hello, attachment; hello, craving. You feel like a tightness in my jaw, a hardness in my belly, and an abusive voice in my mind."

Part 1: Mindfulness of Walking

When walking, know that you are walking—that's the goal of this meditation.

Find a place to walk that is twenty or thirty feet long. Standing at the beginning of the path, bring full attention to the body. Feel the feet firmly planted on the ground. Allow the breath to be natural, and contemplate walking. As you intentionally begin to walk, bring attention to your feet; feel the pressure and movement of each step. Notice the balancing act that the body does as each step shifts the body's weight from side to side. Your hands can fall wherever is easy and natural. Your eyes don't need to be looking at your feet or closed in order to pay attention to the experience of mindful walking; it's usually best to keep them focused a few feet in front of you on the walking terrain.

When the attention is drawn back into thinking about something else, pause and acknowledge that you have lost mindfulness of walking. Note where the attention was drawn and then continue down the path, placing about 80 percent of your attention in the body (especially the feet) and 20 percent on your surroundings. Acknowledge seeing, and note how the mind tends to instantly label all forms: grass, carpet, floor, dirt, and so on.

When you reach the end of the path you have chosen, again pause and feel both feet on the ground. Bringing full attention to the experience of standing, this is now standing meditation. Then intentionally turn around, bringing attention to the balancing act of turning the body, the swiveling of the feet, and the redistribution of weight.

Facing the path you just walked down, begin walking toward the other end. Repeat the process of walking back and forth along this path as a meditative training in present-time awareness. Find a pace that fits your energy and intention of moment-to-moment awareness. Walking slowly may facilitate a more precise experience of the constantly changing physical phenomena of the body. Walking at a normal pace or quickly may be useful for integrating mindfulness into daily life and the fast-paced, busy lives most of us lead.

Part 2: Mindfulness of Eating

Look closely at what you are about to eat. What is it made of? Where did it come from? How many people were involved in the growth, transportation, and preparation of this food? How does your body feel in anticipation of eating? What's happening in your mouth? In your belly? Other sensations?

Take one bite at a time. Bring the food to your mouth. Feel the sensations as it is experienced by the taste buds. Chewing what is in your mouth, pay close attention to what your tongue is doing. Thoroughly chew and swallow what is in your mouth before you take another bite.

Repeat this process over and over with each bite, putting down the fork, spoon, or finger food between bites. In this way we learn to taste, savor, and swallow mindfully. We can watch craving or aversion as it arises in relationship to our food.

If you are having a whole meal, take your time. When you are about halfway through with the food on your plate, stop eating. Pause and bring mindfulness into your body. Wait two or three minutes before you continue. It takes several minutes for the body to register being full or satisfied. But we tend to eat so quickly that by the time the body lets us know it's full, we have already eaten too much.

After pausing, continue. Eat each bite mindfully. Taste it all.

This can and should be done with foods that you like and ones that you don't care for so much. Experiment with eating meditations. Try eating something you love, slowly. Try eating something you don't like, mindfully.

Heart Practices

Compassion Meditation

Find a comfortable place to sit, and allow your attention to settle into the present-time experience of the body. Relax any physical tension that is being held in the body by softening the belly; relax the eyes and jaw and allow your shoulders to naturally fall away from the head.

After a short period of settling into present-time awareness, begin to reflect on your deepest desire for happiness and freedom from suffering. Allow your heart's truest longing for truth and well-being to come into consciousness. With each breath, breathe into the heart's center the acknowledgment of your wish to be free from harm, to be safe and protected, and to experience compassion for all beings.

Slowly begin to offer yourself compassionate phrases with the intention to uncover the heart's sometimes-hidden caring and friendly response. Your phrases can be as simple as the following:

May I learn to care about suffering and confusion.
May I respond with mercy and empathy to pain.
May I be filled with compassion.

If those phrases do not mean anything to you, create your own words to meditate on. Find a few simple phrases that have a compassionate and merciful intention, and slowly begin to offer these well wishes to yourself.

As you sit in meditation repeating these phrases in your mind, the attention will be drawn back, as in mindfulness meditation, into thinking about other things or resisting and judging the practice or your capacity for compassion. It takes a gentle and persistent effort to return to the next phrase each time the attention wanders:

May I learn to care about suffering and confusion. Feel the
breath and the body's response to each phrase.
May I respond with mercy and empathy to pain. Notice
where the mind goes with each phrase.
May I be filled with compassion. Allow the mind and body
to relax into the reverberations of each phrase.

Simply repeat these phrases over and over to yourself like a kind of mantra or statement of positive intention. But don't expect to instantly feel compassionate through this practice. Sometimes all we see is our lack of compassion and the judging mind's resistance. Simply acknowledge what is happening and continue to repeat the phrases, being as friendly and merciful with yourself as possible in the process.

After a few minutes of sending these compassionate phrases to yourself, bring attention back to your breath and body, again relaxing into the posture.

Then bring someone to mind who has been beneficial for you to know or know of, someone who has inspired you or shown you great compassion.

Recognizing that just as you wish to be cared for and understood that your benefactor too shares the universal desire to be met with compassion, begin offering him or her the caring phrases. Slowly repeat each phrase with that person in mind as the object of your well-wishing:

> *Just as I wish to learn to care about suffering and confusion, to*
> *respond with mercy and empathy to pain, and to be filled with*
> *compassion, may you learn to care about suffering and confusion.*
> *May you respond with mercy and empathy to pain.*
> *May you be filled with compassion.*

Continue offering these phrases from your heart to your benefactor's, developing the feeling of compassion in relationship to the pain of others. When the mind gets lost in a story, memory, or fantasy, simply return to the practice. Begin again offering mercy and care to the benefactor.

After a few minutes of sending compassion to the benefactor, let him or her go and return to your direct experience of the breath and body. Pay extra attention to your heart or emotional experience.

Then bring to mind someone whom you do not know well, someone who is neutral. Someone you neither love nor hate—perhaps someone you don't know at all, a person you saw during your day, walking down the street or in line at the market. With the understanding that the desire for freedom from suffering is universal, begin offering that neutral person the compassionate phrases:

> *May you learn to care about suffering and confusion.*
> *May you respond with mercy and empathy to pain.*
> *May you be filled with compassion.*

After a few minutes of sending compassion to the neutral person, bring attention back to your breath and body. Then expand the practice to include family and friends toward whom your feelings may be mixed, both loving and judgmental:

May you all learn to care about suffering and confusion.
May you all respond with mercy and empathy to pain.
May you all be filled with compassion.

After a few minutes of sending compassion to the mixed category, bring attention back to your breath and body. Then expand the practice to include the difficult people in your life and in the world. (By *difficult* we mean those whom you have put out of your heart, those toward whom you hold resentment.)

With even the most basic understanding of human nature, it will become clear that all beings wish to be met with compassion; all beings—even the annoying, unskillful, violent, confused, and unkind—wish to be free from suffering. With this in mind, and with the intention to free yourself from hatred, fear, and ill will, allow someone who is a source of difficulty in your mind or heart to be the object of your compassion meditation, meeting that person with the same phrases and paying close attention to your heart-mind's response:

May you learn to care about suffering and confusion.
May you respond with mercy and empathy to pain.
May you be filled with compassion.

After a few minutes of practice in the direction of difficult people, begin to expand the field of compassion to all those who are in your immediate vicinity. Start by sending compassionate phrases to anyone in your home or building at the time of practice. Then gradually expand to those in your town or city, allowing your positive intention for meeting everyone with compassion to spread out in all directions.

Imagine covering the whole world with these positive thoughts. Send compassion to the north and south, east and west. Radiate an open heart and fearless mind to all beings in existence—those above and below, the seen and the unseen, those being born and those who are dying. With a boundless and friendly intention, begin to repeat the phrases:

> *May all beings learn to care about suffering and confusion.*
> *May all beings respond with mercy and empathy to pain.*
> *May all beings be filled with compassion.*

After a few minutes of sending compassion to all beings everywhere, simply let go of the phrases and bring attention back to your breath and body, investigating the sensations and emotions that are present now. Then, whenever you are ready, allow your eyes to open and your attention to come back to your surroundings.

Tonglen Meditation (A Tibetan Form of Compassion Meditation)

Find a comfortable posture, one that is alert and upright but also relaxed and soft. Allow your eyes to close and bring full attention into your heart center. Allow the breath to feel as though it is entering and exiting directly through the heart.

Begin to reflect on all the greed, hatred, and confusion in this world we live in. Acknowledge how all beings are suffering on some level or another. Some are dying of starvation, some are dying of obesity. Some are suffering from oppression, some are suffering so much that they are oppressing others. Turn your heart and mind toward the truth of suffering in this world.

Now begin to breathe in all the suffering in the world that you are aware of. Allow your heart to open and be filled with the sorrow of the world. Feel that pain, feel the grief, feel the sorrow. Let it all in.

Then breathe it all out, exhale waves of compassion in all directions. Send mercy and forgiveness to all living beings, to the whole world.

Do this over and over. Breathing in the suffering. Breathing out compassion.

After a few minutes of that generalized giving and receiving, begin to add a visual quality to your meditation.

As you breathe in, visualize the pain and suffering as black, heavy, and hot. Breathe in the dark fire of the world's sorrow.

As you exhale, visualize the mercy and compassion as white, light, and cool. Breathe out the soothing, cool, and refreshing intention of compassion.

Continue the hot/cold breathing for a few minutes.

Next we come to the personal aspect of the practice. Bring to mind specific situations in your life that are painful. Breathe into your heart the pain of your life situation, feeling it completely. Breathe out mercy and compassion for yourself.

Over and over: in, suffering; out, compassion.

After a few minutes of the practice with your personal difficulties, begin to expand again. This time include people in your life whom you love. Breathe in the pain and sorrow of your loved ones. See it as heavy, dark, and hot. Breathe out compassion for their sufferings. Experience the out breath as light, white, and cooling.

Breathe in the sorrow. Breathe out loving, caring compassion.

After a few minutes with loved ones, expand to include all the people whom you do not already love. Include the pain and sorrow of the masses and even of your enemies. Everyone is suffering one level or another, just like you.

Breathe in the suffering of humanity. Breathe out compassion for humanity.

Breathe in the pain that closes the heart of our enemies. Breathe out the compassion that heals the wounds that create the unskillful actions of our enemies.

Work with this level for as long as it takes to begin to mean it. Eventually you will sincerely care for the suffering of all living beings, including the most unskillful of your enemies.

Last, we let go of the personal levels of our lives and of the human realm and expand the practice in all directions to include all forms of life. Include animals, insects, birds, fish, and so on. Breathe in the pain and suffering of all living beings. Breathe out compassion and love for all the world.

In, black, heavy, and hot. Out, white, light, and cool.

Remember to include yourself in this last section. You are part of this interconnected web of existence.

After some time, let go of the visualization and just breathe normally. Feel your breath and body. Pay attention to your heart and mind.

Perhaps end the practice with the simple statement: "May I awaken the compassionate heart, for the benefit of all living beings."

Loving-Kindness Meditation

Find a comfortable place to sit, and allow your attention to settle into the present-time experience of the body. Relax any physical tension that is being held in the body by softening the belly; relax the eyes and jaw and allow your shoulders to naturally fall away from the head.

After a short period of settling into present-time awareness, begin to reflect on your deepest desire for happiness and freedom from suffering. Allow your heart's sincere longing for truth and well-being to come into consciousness. With each breath, breathe into the heart's center the acknowledgment of your wish to be free from harm, safe, and protected and to experience love and kindness.

Slowly begin to offer yourself kind and friendly phrases with the intention to uncover the heart's sometimes-hidden loving and kind response. Your phrases can be as simple as the following:

May I be happy.
May I be at ease.
May I be free from suffering.

If those phrases do not mean anything to you, create your own words to meditate on. Find a few simple phrases that have a loving and kind intention, and slowly begin to offer these well wishes to yourself.

As you sit in meditation repeating these phrases in your mind, the attention will be drawn back, as in mindfulness meditation, into thinking about other things or resisting and judging the practice or your capacity for love. It takes a gentle and persistent effort to return to the next phrase each time the attention wanders:

May I be happy. Feel the breath and the
    body's response to each phrase.
May I be at ease. Notice where the mind goes with each phrase.

May I be free from suffering. Allow the mind and body
to relax into the reverberations of each phrase.

Simply repeat these phrases over and over to yourself like a kind
of mantra or statement of positive intention. But don't expect to
instantly feel loving or kind as a result of this practice. Sometimes
all we see is our lack of kindness and the judging mind's resistance.
Simply acknowledge what is happening and continue to repeat the
phrases, being as friendly and merciful with yourself as possible in
the process.

After a few minutes of sending these loving and kind phrases to
yourself, bring attention back to your breath and body, again relaxing into the posture.

Then bring someone to mind who has been beneficial for you
to know or know of, someone who has inspired you or shown you
great kindness. Recognizing that just as you wish to be happy and
at peace and that your benefactor too shares the universal desire
for well-being and love, begin offering him or her these loving and
kind phrases. Slowly repeat each phrase with that person in mind
as the object of your well-wishing:

Just as I wish to be happy, at ease, and free, may you too be happy.
May you be at ease.
May you be free from suffering.

Continue offering these phrases from your heart to your benefactor's, developing the feeling of kindness and response of love to
others. When the mind gets lost in a story, memory, or fantasy,
simply return to the practice. Begin again offering loving-kindness
to the benefactor.

After a few minutes of sending loving-kindness to the benefactor,
let him or her go and return to your direct experience of the breath
and body. Pay extra attention to your heart or emotional experience.

Then bring to mind someone whom you do not know well, someone who is neutral. Someone you neither love nor hate— perhaps someone you don't know at all, a person you saw during your day, walking down the street or in line at the market. With the understanding that the desire for happiness and love is universal, begin offering that neutral person your loving-kindness phrases:

May you be happy.
May you be at ease.
May you be free from suffering.

After a few minutes of sending loving-kindness to the neutral person, bring attention back to your breath and body. Then expand the practice to include family and friends toward whom your feelings may be mixed, both loving and judgmental:

May you be happy.
May you be at ease.
May you be free from suffering.

After a few minutes of sending loving-kindness to the mixed category, bring attention back to your breath and body. Then expand the practice to include the difficult people in your life and in the world. (By *difficult* I mean those whom you have put out of your heart, those toward whom you hold resentment.)

With even the most basic understanding of human nature, it will become clear that all beings wish to be met with love and kindness; all beings—even the annoying, unskillful, violent, confused, and unkind—wish to be happy. With this in mind and with the intention to free yourself from hatred, fear, and ill will, allow someone who is a source of difficulty in your mind or heart to be the object of your loving-kindness meditation.

Meeting that person with the same phrases, pay close attention to your heart-mind's response:

May you be happy.
May you be at ease.
May you be free from suffering.

After a few minutes of practice in the direction of difficult people, begin to expand the field of loving-kindness to all those who are in your immediate vicinity. Start by sending phrases of loving-kindness to anyone in your home or building at the time of practice. Then gradually expand to those in your town or city, allowing your positive intention for meeting everyone with love and kindness to spread out in all directions.

Imagine covering the whole world with these positive thoughts. Send loving-kindness to the north and south, east and west. Radiate an open heart and fearless mind to all beings in existence— those above and below, the seen and the unseen, those being born and those who are dying. With a boundless and friendly intention, begin to repeat the phrases:

May all beings be happy.
May all beings be at ease.
May all beings be free from suffering.

After a few minutes of sending loving-kindness to all beings everywhere, simply let go of the phrases and bring attention back to your breath and body, investigating the sensations and emotions that are present now. Then, whenever you are ready, allow your eyes to open and your attention to come back to your surroundings.

Appreciative Joy Meditation

Find a comfortable place to sit, and allow your attention to settle into the present-time experience of the body. Relax any physical tension that is being held in the body by softening the belly; relax the eyes and jaw and allow the shoulders to naturally fall away from the head.

After a short period of settling into present-time awareness, begin to reflect on your deepest desire for happiness or freedom from suffering. Allow your heart's truest longing for truth and well-being to come into consciousness. With each breath, breathe into the heart's center the acknowledgment and appreciation of the joy and happiness you have experienced in your life.

Slowly begin to offer yourself appreciative and encouraging phrases with the intention to uncover the heart's sometimes hidden response of gratitude. Your phrases can be as simple as the following:

May I learn to appreciate the happiness and joy I experience.
May the joy I experience continue and grow.
May I be filled with gratitude.

If those phrases do not mean anything to you, create your own words to meditate on. Find a few simple phrases that have an appreciative intention and slowly begin to offer these well wishes to yourself.

As you sit in meditation repeating these phrases in your mind, the attention will be drawn, as with mindfulness meditation, back into thinking about other things or resisting and judging the practice or your own capacity for appreciation and gratitude. It takes a gentle and persistent effort to return to the next phrase each time the attention wanders:

May I learn to appreciate the happiness and joy I experience. Feel
the breath and the body's response to each phrase.

May the joy I experience grow. Notice where
   the mind goes with each phrase.
May I be filled with gratitude. Allow the mind and body
   to relax into the reverberations of each phrase.

Simply repeat these phrases over and over to yourself like a kind
of mantra or statement of positive intention. But don't expect to
instantly feel grateful through this practice. Sometimes all we see is
our lack of appreciation and the judging mind's resistance. Simply
acknowledge what is happening and continue to repeat the phrases,
being as friendly and merciful with yourself as possible in the process.

After a few minutes of sending these phrases of appreciation to
yourself, bring the attention back to the breath and body, again
relaxing into the posture.

Then bring someone to mind who has been beneficial for you
to know or know of, who has inspired you or brought joy to your
life. Recognizing that just as you wish to be happy and successful
in life and that your benefactor too shares the universal desire to be
met with encouragement, support, and appreciation, begin offering
him or her the phrases. Slowly repeat each phrase with that person
in mind as the object of your well-wishing:

*Just as I wish to learn to appreciate the happiness and joy
   in life, may you too experience joy, and may you be filled
   with appreciation for your happiness and success.*
May your happiness and joy increase.
May you be successful and met with appreciation.

Continue offering these phrases from your heart to your benefactor's, developing the feeling of appreciation in relationship to
the joy and success of others. When the mind gets lost in a story,
memory, or fantasy, simply return to the practice. Begin again offering appreciation and gratitude to the benefactor.

After a few minutes of sending appreciation to the benefactor, let him or her go and return to your direct experience of the breath and body. Pay extra attention to your heart or emotional experience.

Then bring to mind someone whom you do not know well, someone who is neutral. Someone you neither love nor hate—perhaps someone you don't know at all, a person you saw during your day, walking down the street or in line at the market. With the understanding that the desire for joy is universal, begin offering that person the appreciative phrases:

> *May your happiness and joy increase.*
> *May the joy in your life continue and grow.*
> *May you be successful and met with appreciation.*

After a few minutes of sending appreciation to the neutral person, bring attention to your breath and body. Then expand the practice to include family and friends toward whom your feelings may be mixed, both loving and judgmental:

> *May your happiness and joy increase.*
> *May the joy in your life continue and grow.*
> *May you be successful and met with appreciation.*

After a few minutes of sending appreciation to the mixed category, bring attention back to your breath and body. Then expand the practice to include the difficult people in your life and in the world. (By *difficult* I mean those whom you have put out of your heart, those toward whom you hold resentment.)

With even the most basic understanding of human nature, it will become clear that all beings wish to be met with appreciation; all beings—even the annoying, unskillful, violent, confused, and unkind—wish to experience joy. With this in mind, and with the intention to free yourself from jealousy, fear, and ill will, allow

someone who is a source of difficulty in your mind or heart to be
the object of your appreciation meditation.

Meet that person with the same phrases, paying close attention
to your heart-mind's response:

> *May your happiness and joy increase.*
> *May the joy in your life continue and grow.*
> *May you be successful and met with appreciation.*

After a few minutes of practice in the direction of difficult
people, begin to expand the field of appreciation to all those who
are in your immediate vicinity. Start by sending phrases of appreciation to anyone in your home or building at the time of practice.
Then gradually expand to those in your town or city, allowing
your positive intention for meeting everyone with appreciation to
spread out in all directions. Imagine covering the whole world with
these positive thoughts. Send appreciation to the north and south,
east and west. Radiate gratitude and appreciation to all beings
in existence—those above and below, the seen and the unseen,
those being born and those who are dying. With a boundless and
friendly intention, begin to repeat the phrases of appreciative joy:

> *May your happiness and joy increase.*
> *May the joy in your life continue and grow.*
> *May you be successful and met with appreciation.*

After a few minutes of sending appreciation to all beings
everywhere, simply let go of the phrases and bring attention
back to your breath and body, investigating the sensations and
emotions that are present now. Then, whenever you are ready,
allow your eyes to open and your attention to come back to your
surroundings.

Equanimity Meditation

Find a comfortable place to sit, and allow your attention to settle into the present-time experience of the body. Relax any physical tension that is being held in the body by softening the belly; relax the eyes and jaw, and allow your shoulders to naturally fall away from the head.

After a short period of settling into present-time awareness, begin to reflect on your deepest desire for happiness and freedom from suffering for both yourself and others. Reflect on your desire to serve the needs of others and to be compassionately engaged in the world. Reflect on both the joy and the sorrow that exist in the world. Allow your heart's truest longing for truth and well-being to come into consciousness. With each breath, breathe into the heart's center the acknowledgment of the need to balance your pure intention of creating positive change with the reality of your inability to control others.

Begin repeating the following phrases:

All beings are responsible for their own actions.
Suffering or happiness is created through one's relationship
  to experience, not by experience itself.
The freedom and happiness of others is dependent on
  their actions, not on my wishes for them.

Relax into the reverberations of this balance that harmonizes the heart's deepest desire to help others with the mind's wise response of acknowledging our limitations and powerlessness.

Continue to repeat these phrases for as long as feels appropriate. Perhaps ten to twenty minutes is a good amount of time to start with.

Forgiveness Meditation

For this formal forgiveness practice it may be good to create an altar. It could be just a corner of the room, for example, or a small table where you place some photographs or objects that remind you of your intention to forgive.

Find a comfortable place to sit. Relax into the sitting posture. Take a few moments to settle into the position by intentionally releasing any held tension in your face, neck, shoulders, chest, or abdomen. Bring your attention to the present moment through the breath awareness practice.

After settling into the present-time experience of sitting with awareness of the breath, allow the breath to come and go from your heart's center. Imagine breathing directly in and out of your heart. Feel what is present in your heart-mind and begin to set your intention to let go of the past through letting go of resentments. Say the word *forgiveness* in your mind and acknowledge how it feels to consider letting go.

When you are ready, bring to mind some of the ways that you have harmed others, have betrayed or abandoned them. Include both the intentional and unintentional acts of harm you have participated in. Acknowledge and feel the anger, pain, fear, or confusion that motivated your actions.

Begin to ask for forgiveness from those you have harmed:

I ask for your forgiveness.
Please forgive me for having caused you harm.
I now understand that I was unskillful and that my
actions hurt you, and I ask for your forgiveness.

Pause between each phrase, bringing attention to your heart/mind/body's reactions to these practices. Feel the feelings that arise, or the lack of feeling. Acknowledge the desire to be forgiven.

If the mind gets too lost in the story and begins rationalizing and blaming, simply bring your attention back to the breath and body in the present moment, then continue repeating the phrases:

> *I ask for your forgiveness.*
> *Please forgive me for having caused you harm.*
> *I now understand that I was unskillful and that my*
> *   actions hurt you, and I ask for your forgiveness.*

Spend some time repeating these phrases and reflecting on your past unskillfulness, remembering to soften your belly when it gets tight with judgment or fear.

Relax back into breathing in and out of your heart's center. Take a few moments to let go of the last aspect of the exercise. Then begin to reflect on all the ways in which you have been harmed in this lifetime. Remember that you are attempting to forgive the actors, not the actions, and that just as you have been confused and unskillful at times, those who have hurt you were also suffering or confused. Bring to mind and invite back into your heart those who have caused you harm. With as much mercy and compassion as possible, begin offering forgiveness to those who have harmed you, those whom you have been holding resentment toward, with these same phrases:

> *I forgive you.*
> *I forgive you for all the ways that you have caused me harm.*
> *I now offer you forgiveness, whether the hurt came*
> *   through your actions, thoughts, or words.*
> *I know you are responsible for your actions, and I offer you forgiveness.*

Pause between each phrase, bringing attention to your heart/mind/body's reactions to these practices. Feel the feelings that arise, or the lack of feeling. Acknowledge the desire to forgive. If the mind gets too lost in the story and begins rationalizing and blaming, simply bring the attention back to the breath and body in the present moment, then begin repeating the phrases:

I forgive you.
I forgive you for all the ways that you have caused me harm.
I now offer you forgiveness, whether the hurt came
    through your actions, thoughts, or words.
I know you are responsible for your actions, and I offer you forgiveness.

After some time of asking for forgiveness, let go of the phrases and bring attention back to your direct experience of the present moment, feeling the breath as it comes and goes, softening the belly, and relaxing into the present. Attempt to let go of all levels of this exercise, relaxing back into the experience of your breath at the heart's center.

When you are ready, let go of the reflection on those who have harmed you and bring your awareness back to yourself. Relax back into breathing in and out of your heart's center. Take a few moments to let go of the last aspect of the exercise. When you are ready, begin to reflect on yourself. Acknowledge all the ways that you have harmed yourself. Contemplate your life and your thoughts, feelings, and actions toward yourself. Allow a heartfelt experience of the judgmental and critical feelings you carry toward yourself. Just as we have harmed others, there are so many ways that we have hurt ourselves. We have betrayed and abandoned ourselves many times, through our thoughts, words, and deeds—sometimes intentionally, often unintentionally.

Begin to feel the physical and mental experience of sorrow and grief for yourself and the confusion in your life. Breathing into each moment, with each feeling that arises, soften and begin to invite yourself back into your heart. Allow forgiveness to arise. Picture yourself now, or at any time in your life, and reflect on all the ways in which you have judged, criticized, and caused emotional or physical harm to yourself. With as much mercy and compassion as possible, begin to offer yourself forgiveness, perhaps picturing yourself as a child and inviting the disowned aspects of yourself back into your heart:

> *I forgive you.*
> *I forgive you for all the ways that you have caused me harm.*
> *I now offer you forgiveness, whether the hurt came*
>   *through my actions, thoughts, or words.*
> *I know I am responsible for my actions, and I offer myself forgiveness.*

Pause between each phrase, bringing attention to your heart/ mind/body's reactions to these practices. Feel the feelings that arise, or the lack of feeling. Acknowledge the desire to be forgiven.

If the mind gets too lost in the story and begins rationalizing and blaming, simply bring the attention back to the breath and body in the present moment, then begin repeating the phrases:

> *I forgive you.*
> *I forgive you for all the ways that you have caused me harm.*
> *I now offer you forgiveness, whether the hurt came*
>   *through my actions, thoughts, or words.*
> *I know I am responsible for my actions, and I offer myself forgiveness.*

Send yourself a moment of gratitude for trying to free yourself from the long-held resentments that make life more difficult than it needs to be. When you are ready, allow your eyes to open and attention to come back into the room or space you are in.

Format for Refuge Recovery Meetings

Refuge Recovery is designed to be practiced in community. For this program to be successful, we will need people to start meetings, to create new communities. We offer here the meeting format that we have been using in the pilot meetings in Los Angeles since 2008. We hope that as the program develops and grows, new formats and styles of meetings will be created. Our website www.refugerecovery.org will serve as the centralized information hub, where new meetings and new formats will be listed and posted for download.

Those who want to start a new meeting are asked to do so only if they are willing to host the meeting weekly with a minimum commitment of six months. That means that even if no one shows up for the first few months, they continue to be there at the designated place and time each week. Since this is a new movement, we will need to be patient with the process of attracting and sustaining community. We would prefer that all meetings that are open to the public be held in nonresidential settings, but we also understand that at times meetings in someone's home will be the only option.

When each new meeting is started, we will post the information on the website and list the local contact person for that meeting. We encourage a rotating leadership at the meetings, each secretary and other positions within the group taking six-month commitments. As leadership and contact people change, there will be an easy way to update the site.

All meetings are to collect a donation, and the proceeds from the donations are to be used to support the group paying rent and buying any supplies deemed necessary such as coffee or tea. After a prudent reserve is reached, we ask that excess donations be sent to the Refuge Recovery headquarters to support the infrastructure of the nonprofit. All financial records for Refuge Recovery will be public and posted on our site.

Start a meeting and create a refuge for your community. We will be by your side as the Buddhist Refuge Recovery movement grows and spreads.

WELCOME

Secretary reads:

> *Welcome to the Refuge Recovery weekly group. All are welcome here. Our primary purpose is to offer a Buddhist-inspired path to recovery from addiction of all kinds. Our group recognizes and respects that there are multiple perspectives and multiple approaches to recovery; we are gathered in the spirit of investigation of a Buddhist approach. We do not claim to be the only authority, but we know from direct experience that the path outlined in the Four Truths leads to the end of the suffering that addiction causes. We invite you to investigate and practice these truths and to find out for yourself if they are valuable to your process of recovery.*
>
> *It is the intention of this group to explore Buddhist perspectives on recovery. This group is meant to be a support for recovery, not a*

substitute for your dedicated practice; spiritual growth and recovery require individual effort.

Please turn off your electronic devices.

CLARIFICATION OF FACILITATOR ROLE

Secretary/Facilitator reads:

My name is _____, and I am one of the group's secretaries. My role is nonauthoritative. I am not an empowered Buddhist meditation teacher; I am here to facilitate the group and to lead our discussion.

PREAMBLE

Leader reads:

I have asked _____ to read the Refuge Recovery preamble.

Volunteer reads:

Refuge Recovery is a community of people who are using the practices of mindfulness, compassion, forgiveness, and generosity to heal the pain and suffering that addiction has caused in our lives and the lives of our loved ones. The path of practice that we follow is called the Four Truths of Refuge Recovery.

The Four Truths of Refuge Recovery is a Buddhist-oriented path to recovery from addictions. It has proven successful with addicts and alcoholics who have committed to the Buddhist path of meditation, generosity, kindness, and renunciation.

This is an approach to recovery that understands "All beings have the power and potential to free themselves from suffering."

We feel confident in the power of the Buddha's teachings, if applied, to relieve suffering of all kinds, including the suffering of addiction.

Leader reads:

In an effort to build community and to get to know each other, we start each week by introducing ourselves. There is no need to identify yourself by anything other than your name. My name is _____.

MEDITATION INSTRUCTION

Facilitator/Secretary/Speaker reads:

Please hold your comments and questions during guided meditation. Tonight I have asked _____ to lead the meditation.

Meditation (20 min.)

These instructions are to be read slowly to the group, pausing between instruction to allow each participant to absorb and implement these practices. (Remind the meditation leader to read instructions slowly.)

WEEKLY READING

Volunteer(s) reads:

Four Truths and Eightfold Path of Refuge Recovery.
Or other chosen sections from the book *Refuge Recovery*.

Facilitator/Secretary/Speaker shares on Step/Truth/Fold:
Speaker chooses a Recovery-based topic and shares their experience with this topic, or tells their story of addiction and how Buddhist principles have helped them in the recovery process.

GROUP SHARING

Leader reads:

> *The meeting is now open for sharing; please limit your comments to between 3 and 5 minutes. Try to keep your sharing focused on tonight's topic, or on the relationship of recovery, addiction, and Buddhist principles. Sharing is tag-pass; please pick someone to share when you have finished. If you would like to pass, please tell us your name and pass to someone else.*

(Leader picks first person to share.)

CLOSING READING

Facilitator/Secretary reads (if applicable):
Some leaders may choose a short passage from *Refuge Recovery* to end the meeting with.

IMPORTANCE OF ANONYMITY AND CONFIDENTIALITY

Leader reads:

> *In order for this to be a group where we feel safe to share about our recovery and to create an atmosphere of openness, we ask that who you see here and what you hear here remain confidential.*

ANNOUNCEMENTS

Facilitator/Secretary speaks:
Dana ($5 suggested donation), cleanup, thank set up person, phone/e-mail list. Upcoming retreats or new groups.

DEDICATION OF MERIT

Leader reads:

> *We will close with a dedication of merit. Tonight I have asked*
> _____ *to lead us in our offering.*

(Volunteer reads Dedication of Merit.)

1. Mindfulness of Breathing

Find a comfortable way to sit. Adjust your posture so that your spine is erect without being rigid or stiff. Allow the rest of your body to be relaxed around the upright spine. Rest your hands in your lap or on your legs. Allow your eyes to gently close. Bring full attention to the physical sensations of sitting still.

Pause

Allow your breathing to be natural. Bringing attention to your head, release any tension in the face, soften the eyes, and relax the jaw. Scanning the body slowly downward, relax the neck and shoulders. Feeling the rise and fall of the chest and abdomen with the breath, soften the belly with each exhalation.

Pause

Bringing the attention all the way down through the body to the places of contact with the chair or cushion, allow your body to be supported by the seat you're on. Feel the pressure and density of the relaxed upright body sitting.

Pause

Bringing your full attention to the present-time experience, acknowledge the full range of phenomena that are happening in the moment. Thinking is happening; hearing is happening; seeing (even with the eyes closed), tasting, smelling, and physical and emotional sensations are all present.

Pause

Allowing all the experiences to be as they are, redirect your attention to the sensations of the breath. Let the other sense experiences fall to the background as you bring the awareness of breathing to the foreground.

Pause

Take a few moments to investigate where you feel the breath most easily (usually either at the base of the nostrils or in the rising and falling of the abdomen). Find the place where you feel the breath coming and going, and use that as the point of focus. (It's best to choose one place and stick with it; don't jump back and forth between nose and belly. It is not necessary to follow the breath in and out.)

Two minutes of silence

Breathing in, know that you are breathing in. Breathing out, know that you are breathing out.

Pause

A simple way to stay focused is by quietly acknowledging in your mind, "in" on the inhalation and "out" on the exhalation (if you are paying attention at the nostrils), or "rising" and "falling" (if you are paying attention at the abdomen).

Pause

Of course, you will quickly realize that your attention will not stay with the breath; the attention will be drawn back into thinking over and over. In the beginning, the practice of meditation is often just the practice of training the attention to return to the breath.

Pause

Each time the attention wanders back to the thinking aspect of the mind, gently redirect it back to the breath. (This natural process of training the mind is the essence of meditation.) It is important to understand that this will happen over and over. It doesn't mean that you are doing anything wrong or that you can't meditate. It just means that you, like all people, are so used to thinking about things rather than feeling them that the attention is naturally drawn into thinking again and again.

Two minutes of silence

Bring the attention back to the simple experience of the breath over and over. Breathing in, know that the breath is coming into the body. Breathing out, know that the breath is leaving the body.

Pause

Each time the attention wanders into thinking or to another sense experience, acknowledge that that has happened, noting the thinking or hearing or seeing, and then again return the attention to the awareness of the breath.

Pause

While you are training the mind in present-time awareness of the breath, with the mind's almost constant wandering and returning, it is important to bring a quality of kindness and understanding to the practice.

Pause

Try to be friendly toward your experience. Of course the attention wanders. Try not to take it personally; it's not your fault. That's just what the untrained mind does. It will take some time and perseverance to train the attention to stay with the chosen object of awareness.

Pause

It is necessary to be patient and kind to yourself in the process.

Pause

Easier said than done, I know. But when you get caught (judging yourself, being too critical, or doubting the process), attempt to bring friendliness to your relationship to the thoughts.

Pause

And then simply redirect the attention back to the breath.

Three minutes of silence

(Ring Bell)

2. Mindfulness of the Breath and Body

Find a comfortable way to sit, close your eyes, and relax your body. Bringing attention to the sensations of breath, continue redirecting the attention to the breath each time it wanders. Try to be as friendly and kind as possible to your mind's tendency to wander.

Three minutes of silence

Pause

If you are new to meditation, continue focusing the attention on the breath.

Pause

If you feel ready, begin to expand the attention to the whole body. Bring attention to your posture. Feel the pressure of your body on the cushion or chair. Feel the contact points of your hands touching your legs or resting in your lap. Direct the attention to sensations of sitting.

Pause

With the foundation of present-time awareness, as established by the continual returning of the attention to the breath and body, you can now allow the attention to expand to include all of the sense doors.

Begin with the awareness of hearing. When you become aware of a sound, simply pay attention to the experience of hearing—the bare experience of sound being received by the eardrum.

Pause

Although the mind wants to instantly name the object being heard, the direct experience is just variations of sound. Using memory and conditioning, the mind immediately tries to label the sound as a car passing by, or the wind in the trees.

Pause

In this level of practice, try to see the difference between the direct experience of sound and the mind's conditioned labeling of the experience. Keep it simple; it is just hearing.

Pause

Expand your attention to seeing, tasting, and smelling in the same way. Just seeing and the direct experience of what's being seen—color, shape, form, and so on. Just taste. Just smelling.

Pause

Notice how quickly the mind names and classifies things based on memory. This level of mindfulness allows us to see how the mind is constantly trying to sort and name experiences based on memory, rarely allowing for new or fresh perspectives.

Three minutes of silence

When the attention gets drawn back into thinking, simply return it to the breath. Then continue to extend mindfulness to the direct, moment to moment sensory experience of the whole body.

Pause

Allow the attention to be drawn to whatever experience in the body is predominant. When sounds arise, know them as hearing.

Pause

When visions arise, know them as seeing. Don't settle for the mind's labels and conventions. Experience each moment as if it were the first sensation of its kind ever.

Pause

Bring a childlike interest and curiosity to your present-time experience. What does this moment feel like? What is the temperature, texture, or pressure of this sensory experience?

Pause

Continue to connect the attention with the felt sense of the breath and body. Begin refining the attention to the moment-to-moment flux of sensations. Investigate the constantly changing nature of each experience.

Pause

With clear comprehension receive the transient phenomena with nonjudgmental awareness. Attempt to sustain awareness of the arising and passing of each chosen sensation.

Pause

Continue redirecting the attention and reconnecting with the present moment each time the attention is drawn back into the contents of the thinking mind.

Pause

Attempt to rest in the direct experience of the breath and body, relaxing into the present-time awareness of impermanence.

Two minutes of silence

(Ring Bell)

3. Mindfulness of the Feeling Tone

Find a comfortable way to sit. Adjust your posture so that your spine is erect without being rigid or stiff. Allow the rest of your body to be relaxed around the upright spine. Rest your hands in your lap or on your legs. Allow your eyes to gently close. Bring full attention to the physical sensations of sitting still.

Pause

Allow your breathing to be natural. Bringing attention to your head, release any tension in the face, soften the eyes, and relax the jaw. Scanning the body slowly downward, relax the neck and shoulders. Feeling the rise and fall of the chest and abdomen with the breath, soften the belly with each exhalation.

Pause

Bringing the attention all the way down through the body to the places of contact with the chair or cushion, allow your body to be supported by the seat you're on. Feel the pressure and density of the relaxed upright body sitting.

Pause

Bringing your full attention to the present-time experience, acknowledge the full range of phenomena that are happening in the moment. Thinking is happening; hearing is happening; seeing (even with the eyes closed), tasting, smelling, and physical and emotional sensations are all present.

Pause

Allowing all the experiences to be as they are, redirect your attention to the sensations of the breath. Let the other sense experiences fall to the background as you bring the awareness of breathing to the foreground.

Pause

Take a few moments to investigate where you feel the breath most easily (usually either at the base of the nostrils or in the rising and falling of the abdomen). Find the place where you feel the breath coming and going, and use that as the point of focus. (It's best to choose one place and stick with it; don't jump back and forth between nose and belly. It is not necessary to follow the breath in and out.)

Three minutes of silence

Having establishing some ability to sustain attention, you can now begin to investigate the "feeling tone" of each experience. Whether you are paying attention to the breath or sensations in the body, each experience has a feeling tone of pleasantness, unpleasantness, or neutrality.

Pause

By focusing the attention a little bit more and opening your awareness to the subtle levels of pleasant and unpleasant tones of experience, you bring mindfulness to your craving for pleasure and aversion to pain. Feeling tone is the place where one gets attached or aversive.

Pause

While sitting with awareness focused on the body, refine the attention to the feeling tone of your experience. Investigate and inquire into the nature of the experience you are paying attention to. Is this a pleasant feeling?

Pause

Does it feel good?

Pause

Or is it an uncomfortable experience?

Pause

Are you resisting the present feeling?

Pause

Bring mindfulness to the feeling itself; see for yourself how you relate to pleasure and pain.

What does your mind do when the present-time experience is neutral?

Pause

Are you able to hang out with experiences that have no pleasure or pain associated with them? Or does the mind get bored and seek a pleasurable or painful memory or plan?

Pause

Continue training the mind in this way. Each time the attention wanders, gently return to the present moment and continue investigating your inner relationship to the pleasant, unpleasant, or neutral tone of each moment.

Three minutes of silence

When you become aware of attachment to a pleasurable experience, attempt to let go. Release the mind/body's grip by softening and relaxing into each moment.

Pause

Allow yourself to fully experience and enjoy the pleasure as it comes and goes.

Pause

When you become aware of aversion to an unpleasant experience, attempt to meet it with mercy and friendliness.

Pause

Allow the pain or discomfort to be present, and meet it with the understanding that it will pass if you just allow it to come through the mind/body without trying to resist it, suppress it, or control it.

Pause

When you are meditating on neutral phenomena, attempt to relax into the absence of suffering. Tolerate the mind's craving for pleasure and continue to enjoy the experience of just being.

Pause

Learning to enjoy the absence of pleasure and pain is key on the meditative path.

Two minutes of silence

(Ring Bell)

4. Mindfulness of the Mind

Part 1: Process

Find a comfortable way to sit. Adjust your posture so that your spine is erect without being rigid or stiff. Allow the rest of your body to be relaxed around the upright spine. Rest your hands in your lap or on your legs. Allow your eyes to gently close. Bring full attention to the physical sensations of sitting still.

Pause

Allow your breathing to be natural. Bringing attention to your head, release any tension in the face, soften the eyes, and relax the jaw. Scanning the body slowly downward, relax the neck and shoulders. Feeling the rise and fall of the chest and abdomen with the breath, soften the belly with each exhalation.

Pause

Bringing the attention all the way down through the body to the places of contact with the chair or cushion, allow your body to be supported by the seat you're on. Feel the pressure and density of the relaxed upright body sitting.

Pause

Bringing your full attention to the present-time experience, acknowledge the full range of phenomena that are happening in the moment. Thinking is happening; hearing is happening; seeing (even with the eyes closed), tasting, smelling, and physical and emotional sensations are all present.

Pause

Allowing all the experiences to be as they are, redirect your attention to the sensations of the breath. Let the other sense experiences fall to the background as you bring the awareness of breathing to the foreground.

Pause

Take a few moments to investigate where you feel the breath

most easily (usually either at the base of the nostrils or in the rising and falling of the abdomen). Find the place where you feel the breath coming and going, and use that as the point of focus. (It's best to choose one place and stick with it; don't jump back and forth between nose and belly. It is not necessary to follow the breath in and out.)

Pause

While you are training the mind in present-time awareness of the breath, with the mind's almost constant wandering and returning, it is important to bring a quality of kindness and understanding to the practice.

Pause

Try to be friendly toward your experience. Of course the attention wanders. Try not to take it personally; it's not your fault. That's just what the untrained mind does. It will take some time and perseverance to train the attention to stay with the chosen object of awareness.

Three minutes of silence

From the foundation of present-time investigative awareness that is infused with the intention of kindness and understanding, you can turn your attention on the mind itself.

Pause

After having established awareness of the breath/body and the feeling tone of the present moment, expand the attention to the process of the thinking mind. Observe the arising and passing of thoughts.

Pause

Allow the awareness to be expansive: try not to get caught in the content of the thoughts; let go of the need to solve any problems or make any plans. Just relax into the present-time awareness of thoughts coming and going.

Pause

Break the addiction to the contents of and identification with your mind. Meditate on the mind as a process. Each thought is like a bubble floating through the spaciousness of awareness. One may contain a plan, another a memory, and yet another a judgment or emotion.

Pause

Allow each thought to pass without getting into the bubble or floating off with it.

Three minutes of silence

Until the meditation practice has matured, you will get seduced by the thinking mind over and over, floating off into a plan or memory that feels too important to let pass. Or all of a sudden you will have what seems like the most important revelation or inspiration.

Pause

This is the natural process of training the mind and transforming your relationship to the contents of your mind.

Pause

As with the breath, simply let go and return to the present over and over, bursting the bubble and redirecting the attention to the process again and again.

Pause

If there is a foundation of attention that is concentrated and stable, you may be able to experience the completely impersonal phenomenon of the proliferation of thoughts.

Pause

You may see that one thought that arises leads to the next and the next and the next, until all of a sudden the mind is off in some fantasy, each bubble giving birth to the next.

Two minutes of silence

(Ring Bell)

Part 2: Content

Find a comfortable way to sit. Adjust your posture so that your spine is erect without being rigid or stiff. Allow the rest of your body to be relaxed around the upright spine. Rest your hands in your lap or on your legs. Allow your eyes to gently close. Bring full attention to the physical sensations of sitting still.

Pause

Allow your breathing to be natural. Bringing attention to your head, release any tension in the face, soften the eyes, and relax the jaw. Scanning the body slowly downward, relax the neck and shoulders. Feeling the rise and fall of the chest and abdomen with the breath, soften the belly with each exhalation.

Pause

Bringing the attention all the way down through the body to the places of contact with the chair or cushion, allow your body to be supported by the seat you're on. Feel the pressure and density of the relaxed upright body sitting.

Pause

Bringing your full attention to the present-time experience, acknowledge the full range of phenomena that are happening in the moment. Thinking is happening; hearing is happening; seeing (even with the eyes closed), tasting, smelling, and physical and emotional sensations are all present.

Pause

Allowing all the experiences to be as they are, redirect your attention to the sensations of the breath. Let the other sense experiences fall to the background as you bring the awareness of breathing to the foreground.

Pause

Take a few moments to investigate where you feel the breath most easily (usually either at the base of the nostrils or in the rising and falling of the abdomen). Find the place where you feel the breath coming and going, and use that as the point of focus.

(It best to choose one place and stick with it; don't jump back and forth between nose and belly. It is not necessary to follow the breath in and out.)

Three minutes of silence

Having establishing some ability to sustain attention, you can now begin to investigate the "feeling tone" of each experience. Whether you are paying attention to the breath or sensations in the body, each experience has a feeling tone of pleasantness, unpleasantness, or neutrality.

Pause

By focusing the attention a little bit more and opening your awareness to the subtle levels of pleasant and unpleasant tones of experience, you bring mindfulness to your craving for pleasure and aversion to pain. Feeling tone is the place where one gets attached or aversive.

Pause

While sitting with awareness focused on the body, refine the attention to the feeling tone of your experience. Investigate and inquire into the nature of the experience you are paying attention to. Is this a pleasant, unpleasant, or neutral feeling?

Pause

Having establishing awareness of the breath/body and feeling tones of the present moment, after expanding the attention to the process of the thinking mind and observing the arising and passing of thoughts, bring attention to the contents of each mind moment.

Pause

Know directly the truth of each thought. Be aware of each memory as a memory, and when a plan arises in the mind, know it as a plan—perhaps noting "past" and "future."

Three minutes of silence

Be aware of the arising of all emotion. If fear, anger, sadness, love, caring, envy, empathy, or any other feeling arises, experience it directly; know that it originated in the mind and has manifested in the body as well.

Pause

You may see that fear is an underlying motivator for much of the contents of the mind. See for yourself what is true about your mind.

Pause

Know each experience as it is. Observe the tendency to avoid, suppress, ignore, or resist the unpleasant thoughts, and recognize that as aversion.

Pause

Observe the tendency to cling, crave, and feed the thoughts that are pleasant or that you feel will lead to more safety or happiness, and know that experience as attachment.

Pause

Watch the thoughts. Know the thoughts. But don't get involved.

Three minutes of silence

(Ring Bell)

5. Mindfulness of the Truth

Find a comfortable way to sit. Adjust your posture so that your spine is erect without being rigid or stiff. Allow the rest of your body to be relaxed around the upright spine. Rest your hands in your lap or on your legs. Allow your eyes to gently close. Bring full attention to the physical sensations of sitting still.

Pause

Allow your breathing to be natural. Bringing attention to your head, release any tension in the face, soften the eyes, and relax the jaw. Scanning the body slowly downward, relax the neck and shoulders. Feeling the rise and fall of the chest and abdomen with the breath, soften the belly with each exhalation.

Pause

Bringing the attention all the way down through the body to the places of contact with the chair or cushion, allow your body to be supported by the seat you're on. Feel the pressure and density of the relaxed upright body sitting.

Three minutes of silence

Begin to expand your attention to the whole mind and body. Know your experience as it is. When you become aware of the hindrances of sleepiness, restlessness, craving, aversion, or doubt, simply pay direct attention to the truth of these experiences.

Pause

What does it feel like in the body? Where do you physically experience restlessness, sleepiness, aversion, or craving? Is the experience constant or constantly changing?

Pause

If doubt arises, name it. Explore it. What does doubt feel like in your belly?

Three minutes of silence

Now investigate the factors of awakening:

Is mindfulness present?

One minute of silence

Is the mind concentrated?

One minute of silence

Is the factor of investigation present?

One minute of silence

How is your energy and effort in this moment? Are you awake and present? Do you feel energized or lethargic?

One minute of silence

Is the factor of joy present? How do you experience the joy?

Pause

What kind of sensations are associated with joy?

Pause

What kind of thoughts arise in the mind when joy is present? Are you attached to these thoughts and feelings, or do you let them rise and pass?

One minute of silence

Do you feel equanimous with your mind and body? Are you at ease? Balanced?

Pause

Allow relaxation to arise. Right now, it's just like this, the way it is. Relax around it, into it. Let it be and observe. Investigate and contemplate the truth of each moment as it manifests in the body and mind.

Pause

Remember to keep the intention of objective friendliness. Meet each experience with acceptance and curiosity: "So this is suffering; hello, attachment; hello, craving. You feel like a tightness in my jaw, a hardness in my belly, and an abusive voice in my mind."

Pause

Or "So this is joy; welcome. You feel warm and embracing. Sweet and pleasant. My belly is soft, chest open, and jaw is relaxed."

One minute of silence

We can welcome all the emotions, sensations, and truth of our experience in mindful awareness.

Pause

All that arises, passes.

Pause

There is nothing worth clinging to.

Pause

Let it all come, let it all go.

(Ring Bell)

Eating Meditation

(To do this meditation in the group, first pass out something small and simple to eat, like raisins. Ask each person to take some, but to await further instructions. When every one has received the edible, begin.)

Look closely at what you are about to eat.

Pause

Touch it. Smell it.

Pause

What is it made of?

Pause

Where did it come from?

Pause

Reflect on how many people may have been involved in the growth, transportation, and preparation of this food?

Pause

How does your body feel in anticipation of eating?

Pause

What's happening in your mouth? In your belly? Other sensations?

Pause

When you are ready, bring the food to your mouth. But don't chew it yet. Let your tongue explore it first.

Pause

Feel the sensations as it is experienced by the taste buds.

Pause

As you begin chewing what is in your mouth, pay close attention to what your tongue is doing.

Pause

Thoroughly chew and swallow what is in your mouth before you take another bite.

Pause

In this way we learn to chew, taste, savor, and swallow mindfully. We can watch craving or aversion as it arises in relationship to our food.

Pause

Everything we put in our mouths now becomes an opportunity for meditation.

(Ring Bell)

Compassion Meditation

After establishing a comfortable sitting posture, allow your eyes to close and your attention to settle into the present-time experience of the body. Relax any physical tension that is being held in the body by softening the belly; relax the eyes and jaw and allow your shoulders to naturally fall away from the head.

Pause

After a short period of settling into present-time awareness, begin to reflect on your deepest desire for happiness and freedom from suffering. Allow your heart's truest longing for truth and well-being to come into consciousness.

Pause

With each breath, breathe into the heart's center the acknowledgment of your wish to be free from harm, to be safe and protected, and to experience compassion for all beings.

Pause

Slowly begin to silently offer yourself compassionate phrases with the intention to uncover the heart's sometimes-hidden caring and friendly response. Your phrases can be as simple as the following:

May I learn to care about suffering and confusion.

Pause

May I respond with mercy and empathy to pain.

Pause

May I be filled with compassion.

Pause

If those phrases do not mean anything to you, create your own. Find a few simple phrases that have a compassionate and merciful intention, and slowly begin to offer these well wishes to yourself.

Pause

As you silently repeat these phrases, the attention will be drawn back into thinking of other things or resisting and judging the practice or your capacity for compassion. It takes gentle, persistent effort to return to the next phrase each time the attention wanders:

May I learn to care about suffering and confusion.

Feel the breath and the body's response to each phrase.
Pause

May I respond with mercy and empathy to pain.

Notice where the mind goes with each phrase.
Pause

May I be filled with compassion.

Allow the mind and body to relax into the reverberations of each phrase.
Pause
Simply repeat these phrases over and over to yourself like a kind of mantra or statement of positive intention. But don't expect to instantly feel compassionate through this practice.
Pause
Sometimes all we see is our lack of compassion and the judging mind's resistance. Simply acknowledge this and continue to repeat the phrases, being as merciful with yourself as possible.
Three minutes of silence
Let go of sending compassion to yourself and bring attention back to your breath and body, again relaxing into the posture. Then bring someone to mind who has been beneficial for you to know or someone who has inspired you or shown you compassion.
Pause
Recognizing that just as you wish to be cared for and understood that your benefactor too shares the universal desire to be met with compassion, begin offering him or her the caring phrases.

Slowly repeat each phrase with that person in mind as the object of your well-wishing:

Just as I wish to learn to care about suffering and confusion, to respond with mercy and empathy to pain, and to be filled with compassion, may you also learn to care about suffering and confusion.

Pause

May you respond with mercy and empathy to pain.

Pause

May you be filled with compassion.

Pause

Continue offering these phrases from your heart to your benefactor's, developing the feeling of compassion in relationship to the pain of others. When the mind gets lost in a story, memory, or fantasy, simply return to the practice.

Pause

Begin again offering mercy and care to the benefactor.

Three minutes of silence

Now let the benefactor go and return to your direct experience of the breath and body. Pay extra attention to your heart or emotional experience.

Pause

Then bring to mind someone whom you do not know well, someone who is neutral. Someone you neither love nor hate— perhaps someone you don't know at all, a person you saw during your day, walking down the street or in line at the market.

Pause

With the understanding that the desire for freedom from suffering is universal, begin offering that neutral person the compassionate phrases:

May you learn to care about suffering and confusion.

Pause

May you respond with mercy and empathy to pain.

Pause

May you be filled with compassion.

Three minutes of silence

Now expand the practice to include family and friends toward whom your feelings may be mixed, both loving and judgmental:

May you all learn to care about suffering and confusion.

Pause

May you all respond with mercy and empathy to pain.

Pause

May you all be filled with compassion.

Three minutes of silence

Now expand the practice to include the difficult people in your life and in the world. (By difficult we mean those whom you have put out of your heart, those toward whom you hold resentment.)

With even the most basic understanding of human nature, it will become clear that all beings wish to be met with compassion; all beings—even the annoying, unskillful, violent, confused, and unkind—wish to be free from suffering.

Pause

With this in mind, and with the intention to free yourself from hatred, fear, and ill will, allow someone who is a source of difficulty in your mind or heart to be the object of your compassion meditation, meeting that person with the same phrases and paying close attention to your heart-mind's response:

May you learn to care about suffering and confusion.

Pause

May you respond with mercy and empathy to pain.

Pause

May you be filled with compassion.

Three minutes of silence

Now begin to expand the field of compassion to all those who are in your immediate vicinity. Start by sending compassionate phrases to everyone in the meeting. Then gradually expand to those in your town or city, allowing your positive intention to spread out in all directions.

Pause

Imagine covering the whole world with these positive thoughts. Send compassion to the north and south, east and west. Radiate an open heart and fearless mind to all beings in existence—those above and below, the seen and the unseen, those being born and those who are dying. With a boundless and friendly intention, begin to repeat the phrases:

May all beings learn to care about suffering and confusion.
May all beings respond with mercy and empathy to pain.
May all beings be filled with compassion.

After a few minutes of sending compassion to all beings every-where, simply let go of the phrases and bring attention back to your breath and body, investigating the sensations and emotions that are present now. Then, whenever you are ready, allow your eyes to open and your attention to come back to your surroundings.

Tonglen Meditation

Find a comfortable posture that is alert and upright, but also re-laxed and soft. Allow your eyes to close and bring full attention into your heart center. Allow the breath to feel as though it is en-tering and exiting directly through the heart.

Pause

Begin to reflect on all the greed, hatred, and confusion in this world we live in. Acknowledge how all beings are suffering on some level or another. Some are dying of starvation, some are dying of obesity. Some are suffering from oppression, some are suffering so much that they are oppressing others. Turn your heart and mind toward the truth of suffering in this world.

Pause

Now begin to breathe in all the suffering in the world that you are aware of. Allow your heart to open and be filled with the sorrow of the world. Feel that pain, feel the grief, feel the sorrow. Let it all in.

Pause

Then breathe it all out, exhale waves of compassion in all directions. Send mercy and forgiveness to all living beings, to the whole world.

Pause

Do this over and over. Breathing in the suffering. Breathing out compassion.

Three minutes of silence

Begin to add a visual quality to your meditation.

As you breathe in, visualize the pain and suffering as black, heavy, and hot. Breathe in the dark fire of the world's sorrow.

Pause

As you exhale, visualize the mercy and compassion as white, light, and cool. Breathe out the soothing, cool, and refreshing in-tention of compassion.

Pause

Continue the hot/cold breathing for a few minutes.

Three minutes of silence

Next we come to the personal aspect of the practice, bringing to mind specific situations in your life that are painful. Breathe into your heart the pain of your life situation, feeling it completely. Breathe out mercy and compassion for yourself.

Pause

Over and over, inhale suffering, exhale compassion.

Two minutes of silence

Begin to expand again. This time include people in your life whom you love. Breathe in the pain and sorrow of your loved ones. See it as heavy, dark, and hot. Breathe out compassion for their sufferings. Experience the out breath as light, white, and cooling.

Pause

Breathe in the sorrow. Breathe out loving, caring, compassion.

Two minutes of silence

Now expand to include all the people that you do not already love. Include the pain and sorrow of the masses and even of your enemies. Everyone is suffering on one level or another, just like you.

Pause

Breathe in the suffering of humanity. Breathe out compassion for humanity.

Breathe in the pain that closes the hearts of our enemies. Breathe out the compassion that heals the wounds that create the unskillful actions of our enemies.

Work with this level for as long as it takes to begin to mean it. Eventually you will sincerely care for the suffering of all living beings, including the most unskillful of your enemies.

Two minutes of silence

Last, we let go of the personal levels of our lives and of the human realm and expand the practice in all directions to include all forms of life. Include animals, insects, birds, fish, and so on. Breathe in the pain and suffering of all living beings. Breathe out compassion and love for all the world.

Pause

In—black, heavy, and hot. Out—white, light, and cool.

Pause

Remember to include yourself in this last section. You are part of this interconnected web of existence.

Two minutes of silence

Now, let go of the visualization and just breathe normally. Feel your breath and body. Pay attention to your heart and mind.

Pause

Ending the practice with the simple statement, *May I awaken the compassionate heart, for the benefit of all living beings.*

(Ring Bell)

Loving-kindness Meditation

Find a comfortable way to sit, and allow your eyes to close. Bring attention into the present-time experience of the body.

Pause

Relax any physical tension that is being held in the body by softening the belly; relax the eyes and jaw and allow your shoulders to naturally fall away from the head.

One minute of silence

Begin to reflect on your deepest desire for happiness and freedom from suffering. Allow your heart's sincere longing for truth and well-being to come into your consciousness.

Pause

With each breath, breathe into the heart's center the acknowledgment of your wish to be free from harm, safe and protected, and to experience love and kindness.

Pause

Slowly begin to offer yourself kind and friendly phrases with the intention to uncover the heart's sometimes-hidden loving and kind response. Your phrases can be as simple as the following:

May I be happy.
May I be at ease.
May I be free from suffering.

If those phrases do not mean anything to you, create your own words to meditate on. Find a few simple phrases that have a loving and kind intention, and slowly begin to offer these well wishes to yourself.

Pause

As you sit in meditation repeating these phrases in your mind, the attention will be drawn back into thinking about other things or resisting and judging the practice or your capacity for love. It

takes a gentle and persistent effort to return to the next phrase
each time the attention wanders:

May I be happy.

Feel the breath and the body's response to each phrase.
Pause

May I be at ease.

Notice where the mind goes with each phrase.
Pause

May I be free from suffering.

Allow the mind and body to relax into the reverberations of
each phrase.

Simply repeat these phrases over and over to yourself like a kind
of mantra or statement of positive intention. But don't expect to
instantly feel loving or kind as result of this practice. Sometimes
all we see is our lack of kindness and the judging mind's resistance.
Simply acknowledge what is happening and continue to repeat the
phrases, being as friendly and merciful with yourself as possible in
the process.

Three minutes of silence

Now bring attention back to your breath and body, again relaxing into the posture.

Pause

Now please bring someone to mind who has been beneficial for
you to know or know of, someone who has inspired you or shown
you great kindness. Recognizing that just as you wish to be happy
and at peace and that your benefactor too shares the universal
desire for well-being and love, begin offering her or him the loving
and kind phrases. Slowly repeat each phrase with that person in
mind as the object of your well-wishing:

Just as I wish to be happy, peaceful, and free, may you too be happy.

Pause

May you be at ease.

Pause

May you be free from suffering.

Pause

Continue offering these phrases from your heart to your benefactor's, developing the feeling of kindness and response of love to others. When the mind gets lost in a story, memory, or fantasy, simply return to the practice. Begin again offering loving-kindness to the benefactor.

One minute of silence

Having spent a few minutes sending loving-kindness to the benefactor, let him or her go and return to your direct experience of the breath and body. Pay extra attention to your heart or emotional experience.

Pause

Now expand the practice to include family and friends toward whom your feelings may be mixed, both loving and difficult:

May you be happy.
May you be at ease.
May you be free from suffering.

Two minutes of silence

Now bring attention back to your breath and body again. Then expand the practice to include the difficult people in your life and in the world. (By difficult we mean those whom you have put out of your heart, those toward whom you hold resentment.)

With even the most basic understanding of human nature, it will become clear that all beings wish to be met with love and kindness; all beings—even the annoying, unskillful, violent, confused, and unkind—wish to be happy.

Pause

With this in mind and with the intention to free yourself from hatred, fear, and ill will, allow someone who is a source of difficulty in your mind or heart to be the object of your loving-kindness meditation.

Pause

Meeting the difficult person with the same phrases:

May you be happy.
May you be at ease.
May you be free from suffering.

Two minutes of silence

Now let's begin to expand the field of loving-kindness to all those who are in our immediate vicinity. Start by sending phrases of loving-kindness to everyone in this room. Then gradually expand to those in our town or city, allowing your positive intention for meeting everyone with love and kindness to spread out in all directions.

Pause

Imagine covering the whole world with these positive thoughts. Send loving-kindness to the north and south, east and west.

Pause

Radiate an open heart and fearless mind to all beings in existence—those above and below, the seen and the unseen, those being born and those who are dying. With a boundless and friendly intention, begin to repeat the phrases:

May all beings be happy.

Pause

   May all beings be at ease.

Pause

   May all beings be free from suffering.

Two minutes of silence

Now let go of the phrases and bring attention back to your breath and body, investigating the sensations and emotions that are present now. Then, whenever you are ready, allow your eyes to open and your attention to come back to your surroundings.

(Ring Bell)

Appreciative Joy Meditation

Find a comfortable way to sit, and allow your eyes to close. Bring attention into the present-time experience of the body.

Pause

Relax any physical tension that is being held in the body by softening the belly; relax the eyes and jaw and allow your shoulders to naturally fall away from the head.

Pause

After a short period of settling into present-time awareness, begin to reflect on your deepest desire for happiness or freedom from suffering. Allow your heart's truest longing for truth and well-being to come into consciousness.

Pause

With each breath, breathe into the heart's center the acknowledgment and appreciation of the joy and happiness you have experienced in your life.

Pause

Slowly begin to silently offer yourself appreciative and encouraging phrases with the intention to uncover the heart's sometimes-hidden response of gratitude. Your phrases can be as simple as the following:

May I learn to appreciate the happiness and joy I experience.

Pause

May the joy I experience continue and grow.

Pause

May I be filled with gratitude and nonattached appreciation.

If those phrases do not mean anything to you, create your own words to meditate on. Find a few simple phrases that have an appreciative intention, and slowly begin to offer these well wishes to yourself.

Pause

As you sit in meditation repeating these phrases in your mind, the attention will be drawn, as with mindfulness meditation, back into thinking about other things or resisting and judging the practice or your own capacity for appreciation and gratitude. It takes a gentle and persistent effort to return to the next phrase each time the attention wanders:

Pause

May I learn to appreciate the happiness and joy I experience.

Feel the breath and the body's response to each phrase.

Pause

May the joy I experience grow.

Notice where the mind goes with each phrase.

Pause

May I be filled with gratitude and nonattached appreciation.

Pause

Allow the mind and body to relax into the reverberations of each phrase.

Simply repeat these phrases over and over to yourself like a kind of mantra or statement of positive intention. But don't expect to instantly feel grateful through this practice. Sometimes all we see is our lack of appreciation and the judging mind's resistance.

Pause

Simply acknowledge what is happening and continue to repeat the phrases, being as friendly and merciful with yourself as possible in the process.

Two minutes of silence

Now bring the attention back to the breath and body, again relaxing into the posture.

Then bring someone to mind who has been beneficial for you to know or know of, who has inspired you or brought joy to your life.

Pause

Recognize that just as you wish to be happy and successful in life and that your benefactor too shares the universal desire to be met with encouragement, support, and appreciation, begin offering him or her the phrases. Slowly repeat each phrase with that person in mind as the object of your well-wishing:

Just as I wish to learn to appreciate the happiness and joy in life, may you too experience joy, and may you be filled with appreciation for your happiness and success.

Pause

May your happiness and joy increase.

Pause

May you be successful and met with appreciation.

Pause

Continue offering these phrases from your heart to your benefactor's, developing the feeling of appreciation in relation to the joy and success of others. When the mind gets lost in a story, memory, or fantasy, simply return to the practice. Begin again offering appreciation and gratitude to the benefactor.

Two minutes of silence

Now let the benefactor go and return to your direct experience of the breath and body. Pay extra attention to your heart or emotional experience.

Pause

Then bring to mind someone whom you do not know well,

someone who is neutral. Someone you neither love nor hate—perhaps someone you don't know at all, a person you saw here today, or walking down the street or in traffic. With the understanding that the desire for joy is universal, begin offering that person the appreciative phrases:

May your happiness and joy increase.
May the joy in your life continue and grow.
May you be successful and met with appreciation.

Two minutes of silence
Now bring attention back to your breath and body. Then expand the practice to include family and friends toward whom your feelings may be mixed, both loving and at times difficult:

May your happiness and joy increase.
May the joy in your life continue and grow.
May you be successful and met with appreciation.

Two minutes of silence
Now bring attention back to your breath and body. Then expand the practice to include the difficult people in your life and in the world. (By difficult we mean those whom you have put out of your heart, those toward whom you feel jealous of or hold resentment.)
Pause
With even the most basic understanding of human nature, it will become clear that all beings wish to be met with appreciation; all beings—even the annoying, unskillful, violent, confused, and greedy—wish to experience joy. With this in mind, and with the intention to free yourself from jealousy, fear, and ill will, allow someone who is a source of difficulty in your mind or heart to be the object of your appreciation meditation.
Pause

Meet that person with the same phrases, paying close attention to your heart-mind's response:

May your happiness and joy increase.
May the joy in your life continue and grow.
May you be successful and met with appreciation.

Two minutes of silence
Now let's begin to expand the field of appreciation to all those who are in your immediate vicinity. Start by sending phrases of appreciation to everyone in the room with us. Then gradually expand to those in our town or city, allowing your positive intention of meeting everyone with appreciation to spread out in all directions.
Pause
Imagine covering the whole world with these positive thoughts. Send appreciation to the north and south, east and west. Radiate gratitude and appreciation to all beings in existence—those above and below, the seen and the unseen, those being born and those who are dying. With a boundless and friendly intention, begin to repeat the phrases of appreciative joy:

May all beings experience happiness and joy.
May the joy in this world continue and grow.
May all beings be successful and met with appreciation.

Two minutes of silence
Now it is time to let go of the phrases and bring attention back to your breath and body, investigating the sensations and emotions that are present now. Then, whenever you are ready, allow your eyes to open and your attention to come back to your surroundings.
(Ring Bell)

Equanimity Meditation

Find a comfortable way to sit, and allow your attention to settle into the present-time experience of the body. Closing your eyes, begin to relax any physical tension that is being held in the body by softening the belly; relax the eyes and jaw and allow your shoulders to naturally fall away from the head.

Pause

After a short period of settling into present-time awareness, begin to reflect on your deepest desire for happiness and freedom from suffering for both yourself and others. Reflect on your desire to serve the needs of others and to be compassionately engaged in the world. Reflect on both the joy and the sorrow that exist in the world.

Two minutes of silence

Allow your heart's truest longing for truth and well-being to come into consciousness. With each breath, breathe into the heart's center the acknowledgment of the need to balance your pure intention of creating positive change with the reality of your inability to control others.

Begin repeating the following phrases:

All beings are responsible for their own actions.

Pause

Suffering or happiness is created through one's relationship to experience, not by experience itself.

Pause

The freedom and happiness of others is dependent on their actions, not on my wishes for them.

Pause

Relax into the reverberations of this balance between harmonizing the heart's deepest desire to help others with the mind's wise response of acknowledging our limitations and powerlessness. Continue to repeat these phrases.

All beings are responsible for their own actions.

Pause

Suffering or happiness is created through one's relationship to experience, not by experience itself.

Pause

The freedom and happiness of others is dependent on their actions, not on my wishes for them.

Three minutes of silence
Stay as consistent and present as possible. Each time you get lost in thoughts or fantasy, come back to the present and return to the phrases.

All beings are responsible for their own actions.

Pause

Suffering or happiness is created through one's relationship to experience, not by experience itself.

Pause

The freedom and happiness of others is dependent on their actions, not on my wishes for them.

Five minutes of silence

All beings are responsible for their own actions.

Pause

Suffering or happiness is created through one's relationship to experience, not by experience itself.

Pause

The freedom and happiness of others is dependent on their actions, not on my wishes for them.

Pause

As we end this meditation, let go of the phrases and bring attention back to your breath and body, investigating the sensations and emotions that are present now. Then, whenever you are ready, allow your eyes to open and your attention to come back to your surroundings.

(Ring Bell)

Refuge Recovery is a nonprofit organization. It is our vision and intention to build an extensive and comprehensive network of Refuge Recovery meetings, communities, and treatment options. We are actively seeking donations to build treatment centers with both residential and outpatient services. Our goal is to raise the capital to start treatment centers through tax-deductible donations, so that all the profit that comes from these services can go back into the community in the form of reduced rates for residential treatment for those without insurance coverage, as well as to scholarships to meditation retreats, access to outpatient services, and building of the infrastructure of the nonprofit. Please consider making a tax-deductible donation at www.refugerecovery.org.